FRANCE

THROUGH

THE AGES

A Concise Guide

By

Martin Miller-Yianni

COPYRIGHT AND ACKNOWLEDGEMENTS

Publisher: Martin Miller-Yianni, Yambol, Bulgaria

First Printing Edition 2024

ISBN 978-619-7742-47-3 (paperback)
ISBN 978-619-7742-48-0 (ePub)

A CIP catalogue record for this book is available from:

The National Register of Published Books in Bulgaria
bulevard 'Vasil Levski' 88,
1504 Sofia,
Bulgaria

Cover Design: By The Author

Title Page Image: 'Marianne' (www.bing.com)

"France Through the Ages: A Concise Guide" presents a true reflection of France's storied past. This book is part of a series of books about the history of various countries. All books in the series are authored with attention to detail and steadfast commitment to accuracy, this account transcends through academic thoroughness, whilst remaining accessible to readers on all levels.

The strength of this book lies in its comprehensive yet detailed exploration of France's history. Each section probes into the intricacies of France's varied historical periods, offering readers lucid insights into the forces that have moulded the nation across centuries.

The author navigates the transitions between historical periods with finesse, providing summaries and clarifications of crucial events that not only maintain the continuity of France's historical narrative but also assist readers in contextualising the grand historical maze.

Whether one is intent on deepening their grasp of specific historical intervals or acquiring an overarching comprehension of France's historical journey, this time provides an abundance of dependable knowledge and astute analysis. Spanning from the achievements and tribulations of ancient societies to the cultural evolutions of recent times, each chapter plunges readers into the story of France's historical development through to its contemporary state.

CONTENTS

Copyright and Acknowledgements i

Introduction ii

The State Emblem of France iv

The Flag of France v

The Location of France vii

Chapter 1 - Prehistoric and Ancient France 1

Chapter 2 - Roman Gaul 9

Chapter 3 - The Merovingian and Carolingian Dynasties 16

Chapter 4 - The Capetian and Medieval France 23

Chapter 5 - The Renaissance and the Valois Dynasty 32

Chapter 6 - The Bourbons and Absolute Monarchy 41

Chapter 7 - The Age of Revolution and Napoleon 51

Chapter 8 - The 19th Century – Restoration to Republic 61

Chapter 9 - The Third Republic and World Wars 70

Chapter 10 - Post-War France and the Fifth Republic 83

Chapter 11 - Contemporary France 93

Chapter 12 - Colonial Legacy to Contemporary Leadership 104

Leaders and Rulers of France 114

Heritage and Traditions of France 120

France's Pioneers in Arts and Entertainment 123

Legends of French Sport 127

Index 130

Illustration and Photo Credits 132

Other Books by the Author 133

The state emblem of France was officially established in 1953, featuring a distinctive design: a blue oval background adorned with a golden bundle of lictors. Within this bundle, the golden axe faces left and is bound by golden ribbons. A prominent golden ribbon bears the national motto of France, "Liberté, Egalité, Fraternité" (Liberty, Equality, Fraternity). Surrounding the lictor bundle are oak and olive branches. The oval itself is encircled by the Grand Master's chain of the Legion of Honour.

This emblem, described by the French Ministry of Foreign Affairs since 1922 and earlier versions dating back to 1905, became particularly prominent during Jacques Chirac's presidency from 1995 onwards.

Historically, following the French Revolution, all symbols associated with the monarchy were discarded, resulting in France being the sole European nation without a traditional national coat of arms. The current emblem, initially introduced in 1905 and enhanced in 1953 with the addition of the Legion of Honour chain, symbolises the nation's republican values and heritage.

The French flag, known as the Tricolour or le drapeau tricolore, is one of the oldest national flags globally. Its origins trace back to the French Revolution in the late 18th century, symbolising the values of the Revolution: liberty, equality, and fraternity. Here is a detailed account of its history, design, and significance:

Historical Background

The origins of the flag are rooted in the French Revolution of 1789. It was first adopted on 15th February 1794 as a symbol of the Republic, replacing the previous royalist flags. The Tricolour design was inspired by the cockades worn by revolutionaries, combining the traditional colours of Paris—blue and red—with white, a symbol of the monarchy.

Design and Specifications

The flag comprises three vertical bands of equal width: blue on the hoist side, white in the middle, and red on the fly side. The blue and red represent the colours of Paris, while the white denotes the monarchy's absolute rule that was being overturned by the Revolution. The precise shades of blue and red have evolved over time, with Pantone 301 for blue and Pantone 186 for red now standardised.

Symbolism

The Tricolour is a potent symbol of French nationalism, embodying the ideals of the Revolution—liberty, equality, and fraternity. It represents the unity and indivisibility of the French nation. The flag is prominently displayed on public buildings, during national holidays like Bastille Day (14th July), and at international events representing France.

Contemporary Use

As the national flag of France, the Tricolour holds official status and is flown throughout the country on government buildings, schools, and private residences. It is also used in international contexts to represent French interests and identity.

Legal Status

The use and display of the French flag are governed by national laws and protocols, ensuring its respectful and appropriate use on public and official occasions. Guidelines exist for its display alongside other flags, particularly within government settings and diplomatic missions.

Influence

The design of the Tricolour has influenced numerous other national flags and symbols worldwide. Its tri-band structure has been adopted by several countries in Europe, Africa, and the Americas, reflecting historical ties or democratic principles inspired by the French Revolution.

The French flag, with its rich history and enduring symbolism, remains a powerful emblem of France's revolutionary heritage and national unity.

THE LOCATION OF FRANCE

France, situated in Western Europe, is known for its diverse landscapes and rich cultural heritage. Geographically, it shares borders with several countries: to the northeast lie Belgium, Luxembourg, Germany, Switzerland, and Italy to the southeast. Spain borders France to the southwest, while the principality of Andorra and the small country of Monaco are nestled within the French mountains along the southern coast.

The geography of France is notably varied. In the north, the country extends to the English Channel and the North Sea, where the landscape is primarily flat, punctuated by gentle hills and valleys. Moving southwards, the terrain becomes more varied and elevated. The central regions of France are dominated by the Massif Central, a mountainous area with volcanic origins, characterised by rugged landscapes and extensive plateaus.

To the east, the French Alps form a natural border with Italy and offer some of Europe's highest peaks, including Mont Blanc, which stands at 4,810 metres (15,781 ft). This mountain range provides excellent skiing and mountaineering opportunities and is renowned for its scenic beauty.

In the south of France, the landscape transitions into the Mediterranean region, characterised by a mild climate, olive groves, vineyards, and picturesque coastal towns. The French Riviera, or Côte d'Azur, stretches along the Mediterranean coast and is famous for its glamorous resorts such as Nice, Cannes, and Saint-Tropez.

France's geography also includes various river systems, the most famous being the Seine, which flows through Paris, and the Loire, known for its châteaux and vineyards. These rivers have historically played a crucial role in the country's economy and culture.

Overall, France's geographical diversity, from its coastal plains to its alpine peaks and volcanic plateaus, contributes to its appeal as a destination rich in natural beauty and cultural heritage.

CHAPTER 1

PREHISTORIC AND ANCIENT FRANCE

Prehistory – 52 B.C.

The history of France begins in the depths of prehistory, with human presence dating back to the Palaeolithic era. Early human inhabitants, belonging to the species Homo erectus, settled in the region over a million years ago. These early settlers were primarily hunter-gatherers, relying on the abundant natural resources for sustenance. Evidence of their presence is scattered across France, with notable sites including the Grotte du Vallonnet near Monaco and the Abri de Cro-Magnon in the Dordogne region.

As the Palaeolithic era progressed, modern Homo sapiens emerged, marking a significant evolution in human culture and technology. The Upper Palaeolithic period, around 40,000 to 10,000 B.C., saw the development of sophisticated tools and the creation of some of the most remarkable prehistoric art known to humanity.

Cave Paintings in Lascaux

One of the most extraordinary examples of early human creativity is found in the cave paintings of Lascaux, located in the

Dordogne Valley. Discovered in 1940 by four teenagers, the Lascaux Cave is adorned with over 600 parietal wall paintings. These artworks, estimated to be around 17,000 years old, predominantly depict large animals such as horses, deer, bison, and aurochs, reflecting the importance of these creatures to the Palaeolithic people.

THE LASCAUX CAVE PAINTINGS

The Lascaux paintings are not merely representations of animals; they reveal a complex understanding of the natural world and the use of symbolism. The artists employed a variety of techniques, including engraving and the use of natural pigments like ochre and charcoal, to create vivid and dynamic images. The significance of these paintings extends beyond their artistic value, offering insights into the spiritual and ritualistic aspects of early human societies.

Transition to the Neolithic Era

The Neolithic era, beginning around 6,000 B.C., marked a profound transformation in human life with the advent of agriculture. This transition from nomadic hunter-gatherer societies to settled farming communities led to the development of permanent villages and the domestication of plants and animals. Neolithic settlements have been discovered across France, with notable sites including the ancient village of Carnac in Brittany, famous for its alignment of megalithic stones known as menhirs.

MEGALITHIC STONES IN THE VILLAGE OF CARNAC (BRITTANY)

The construction of megalithic structures during the Neolithic period is a testament to the increasing social complexity and technological advancement of these early communities. The Carnac stones, consisting of over 3,000 standing stones, are believed to have served religious or astronomical purposes, though their exact function remains a subject of debate among archaeologists.

The Rise of the Gauls

By the end of the Neolithic times, the Celtic culture began to emerge in what is now France. The Celts, an Indo-European people, migrated into the region around 800 B.C., bringing with them new cultural practices, languages, and technologies. This period, known as the Iron Age, saw the rise of the Gauls, who established a vibrant and diverse society across Gaul, the Roman name for the region encompassing modern-day France, Belgium, Luxembourg, and parts of Switzerland, Italy, the Netherlands, and Germany.

Culture and Society

The Gauls were organised into numerous tribes, each with its own territory, leadership, and customs. Despite their tribal divisions, the Gauls shared a common culture, characterised by a warrior aristocracy, complex social structures, and a rich oral tradition preserved by the druids, the learned class responsible for religious and legal matters.

GAUL FORTIFICATION SITE IN BIBRACTE (MONT BEUVRAY)

The Gauls were skilled metalworkers, known for their intricate jewellery, weapons, and tools crafted from iron and bronze. Their settlements, often fortifications, were centres of trade and craftsmanship. Notable fortifications include Bibracte, located on Mont Beuvray, and Gergovia, near present-day Clermont-Ferrand. These fortified towns served as political and economic hubs, reflecting the hierarchical nature of Gallic society.

The Roman Conquest

The Roman conquest of Gaul, initiated by Julius Caesar in 58 B.C., marked the end of Gallic independence and the beginning of a new era in the region's history. The Gallic Wars, documented in Caesar's "Commentarii de Bello Gallico," provide a detailed account of the Roman campaign and the complex interplay of diplomacy, warfare, and local politics.

ROMAN EMPEROR JULIUS CAESAR

The fall of Alesia and the subsequent Roman victory in 52 B.C. signalled the incorporation of Gaul into the Roman Republic. This conquest brought profound changes to Gallic society, including the introduction of Roman law, infrastructure, and culture. The fusion of Gallic and Roman traditions would eventually give rise to the Gallo-Roman civilisation, laying the foundation for the future development of France.

CAESAR'S "COMMENTARII DE BELLO GALLICO"

SUMMARY

The prehistoric and ancient history of France is a complex system of human ingenuity, cultural evolution, and social complexity. From the early Palaeolithic settlers and their stunning cave art to the rise of the Celts and the eventual Roman conquest, each era contributed to the rich and diverse heritage of the region.

PEOPLE:

Homo erectus (over a million years ago) - Early human inhabitants of France during the Palaeolithic era, primarily hunter-gatherers.

Homo sapiens (around 40,000 to 10,000 B.C.) - Early modern humans who created sophisticated tools and remarkable cave art in France.

Vercingetorix (c. 82 B.C. - 46 B.C.) - A Gallic chieftain of the Arverni tribe who led a major revolt against Julius Caesar during the Gallic Wars. He united various Gallic tribes but was eventually defeated at the Battle of Alesia in 52 B.C.

PLACES:

Lascaux Cave (discovered in 1940) - Located in the Dordogne Valley, famous for its stunning Palaeolithic cave paintings dating back around 17,000 years. Depictions include large animals such as horses, deer, bison, and aurochs.

Carnac (Neolithic period) - An ancient village in Brittany known for its alignment of megalithic stones (menhirs), believed to have religious or astronomical significance.

Gergovia (Iron Age) - An oppidum near present-day Clermont-Ferrand, significant during the Gallic Wars and the resistance against Julius Caesar.

EVENTS:

Gallic Wars (58 B.C. - 50 B.C.) - Initiated by Julius Caesar to conquer Gaul (modern-day France and neighbouring regions). The wars culminated in the Battle of Alesia in 52 B.C., where Caesar's forces defeated Vercingetorix's united Gallic tribes.

Roman Conquest of Gaul (58 B.C. - 52 B.C.) - Julius Caesar's successful campaign that led to the incorporation of Gaul into the Roman Republic, introducing Roman law, culture, and infrastructure to the region.

Battle of Alesia (52 B.C.) - A pivotal battle during the Gallic Wars where Julius Caesar's forces besieged Vercingetorix and his Gallic allies, resulting in a decisive Roman victory.

CHAPTER 2

ROMAN GAUL

52 B.C. – 476 A.D.

The Roman conquest of Gaul, led by Julius Caesar, is one of the most significant events in the history of ancient France. From 58 to 50 B.C., Caesar embarked on a series of military campaigns, known as the Gallic Wars, which brought the vast territory of Gaul under Roman control.

Caesar's campaigns were driven by a combination of personal ambition, political manoeuvring, and Rome's strategic interests. Gaul, inhabited by various Celtic tribes, was seen as both a potential threat and an opportunity for expansion. Caesar's narrative of the Gallic Wars, documented in his work "Commentarii de Bello Gallico", as mentioned in the previous chapter, portrays the Gauls as fierce warriors but ultimately highlights the superiority and inevitability of Roman domination.

The initial phase of the conquest involved defeating the Helvetii, a migrating tribe, and repelling incursions by the Germanic leader Ariovistus. Caesar then turned his attention to subjugating the various Gallic tribes. The campaigns were marked by significant battles, such as the Battle of Bibracte in 58 B.C. and the Siege of Alesia in 52 B.C., where Caesar's forces, through tactical brilliance and engineering prowess, besieged and defeated the Gallic chieftain Vercingetorix.

MODERN RECREATION OF ROMAN ALESIA FORTIFICATIONS

The fall of Alesia and the capture of Vercingetorix effectively ended major resistance in Gaul. By 50 B.C., the Roman legions had subdued the region, and Gaul was incorporated into the Roman Republic. The conquest brought about profound changes, setting the stage for the process of Romanisation that would follow.

Romanisation

Following the conquest, the process of Romanisation transformed Gaul into a fully integrated part of the Roman Empire. This period saw the widespread adoption of Roman culture, language, laws, and infrastructure, fundamentally reshaping Gallic society.

Integration into the Roman Empire was facilitated by a combination of military presence, administrative reorganisation, and cultural assimilation. Roman governors were appointed to oversee the provinces of Gaul, ensuring loyalty to Rome and implementing Roman law. The local elite, including many of the former tribal leaders, were co-opted into the Roman system, often being granted Roman citizenship and positions of authority.

The development of cities and infrastructure was a cornerstone of Romanisation. The Romans established and expanded cities (known as civitates), which became centres of administration, commerce, and culture. Notable cities included Lugdunum (modern Lyon), which served as the capital of Roman Gaul, and other major urban centres like Lutetia (Paris), Arelate (Arles), and Massilia (Marseille).

MAP OF ROMAN GAUL (C. 55-50 B.C.)

Roman cities were characterised by their infrastructure and architectural advancements. The construction of roads, aqueducts, and public buildings facilitated economic integration and communication across the vast territory. The Via Agrippa, a network of roads connecting Lugdunum with other parts of Gaul, exemplified the importance of infrastructure in maintaining Roman control and fostering trade.

A ROMAN SITE IN LUGDUNUM (MODERN LYON)

Public amenities such as baths, theatres, amphitheatres, and forums became common in Gallic cities, reflecting the spread of Roman culture. These structures not only served practical purposes but also reinforced the Roman way of life and social norms among the local population.

The adoption of the Latin language played a crucial role in unifying Gaul under Roman rule. Latin became the lingua franca of administration, education, and commerce, gradually replacing the local Celtic languages. Over time, the Latin spoken in Gaul evolved, laying the foundations for the development of the French language.

Economically, Gaul became an important part of the Roman Empire, contributing agricultural products, minerals, and manufactured goods. The integration into the Roman economy brought prosperity to many regions, fostering urban growth and enhancing the standard of living for many inhabitants.

Religion in Roman Gaul underwent significant changes as well. The Roman pantheon was introduced, and traditional Gallic deities were often syncretised with Roman gods. Over time, Christianity spread through the region, particularly from the 3rd century onwards, culminating in the eventual Christianisation of Gaul.

The decline of the Western Roman Empire in the 5th century marked the end of Roman rule in Gaul. In 476 A.D., the deposition of the last Roman emperor in the West signified the collapse of central Roman authority. The region saw the emergence of various Germanic kingdoms, most notably the Franks, who would go on to shape the future of France.

The period of Roman Gaul was marked by the dramatic transformation of the region from a collection of independent Celtic tribes to a fully integrated and Romanised part of the Roman Empire. The legacy of this era, seen in the enduring influence of Roman culture, language, and infrastructure, continues to shape the historical and cultural landscape of modern France.

SUMMARY:

The period of Roman Gaul was marked by the dramatic transformation of the region from a collection of independent Celtic tribes to a fully integrated and Romanised part of the Roman Empire. The legacy of this era, seen in the enduring influence of Roman culture, language, and infrastructure, continues to shape the historical and cultural landscape of modern France.

People:

Julius Caesar (100 B.C. - 44 B.C.) - Conquered Gaul in the Gallic Wars (58-50 B.C.), laying the foundation for Roman control.
Vercingetorix (82 B.C. - 46 B.C.) - Gaulish chieftain who led a major revolt against Caesar in 52 B.C.
Augustus Caesar (63 B.C. - 14 A.D.) - First Roman emperor, who oversaw the incorporation of Gaul into the Roman Empire.

PLACES:

Lugdunum (Lyon) - Founded as a Roman colony in 43 B.C., it became a major administrative centre in Gaul.
Alesia - Site of the decisive battle in 52 B.C. where Julius Caesar defeated Vercingetorix, leading to Roman control over Gaul.
Colonia Agrippina (Cologne) - Established as a Roman colony on the Rhine, a key military and economic centre in Germania Inferior.

EVENTS:

Gallic Wars (58-50 B.C.) - Julius Caesar's campaigns to conquer Gaul, ultimately bringing it under Roman control.
Foundation of Roman Gaul - Gaul was gradually transformed into **Roman Provinces** (Gallia Narbonensis, Gallia Aquitania, Gallia Lugdunensis) between 121 B.C. and 22 B.C.
Migration Period (4th-5th century A.D.) - Beginning with invasions by Germanic tribes such as the Franks and Visigoths, leading to the decline of Roman control and the eventual fall of the Western Roman Empire in 476 A.D.

CHAPTER 3

THE MEROVINGIAN AND CAROLINGIAN DYNASTIES

476 A.D. - 987

The fall of the Western Roman Empire in 476 A.D. marked the beginning of a new era in Gaul, characterised by the rise of the Franks, a Germanic tribe that would come to dominate the region. The Merovingian dynasty, named after the semi-legendary Merovech, laid the foundation for this transformation.

Clovis I, who reigned from approximately 481 to 511 A.D., is credited with uniting the Frankish tribes and establishing the Frankish Kingdom as a major power in Western Europe. Clovis, the son of Childeric I, became king of the Salian Franks and quickly expanded his territory through a combination of military conquest and strategic alliances.

One of Clovis's most significant achievements was his victory over the Roman commander Syagrius at the Battle of Soissons in 486 A.D., which secured northern Gaul for the Franks. He further consolidated his power by defeating other Germanic tribes, such as the Alemanni at the Battle of Tolbiac in 496 A.D.

CLOVIS I LEADING THE FRANKS TO VICTORY IN THE TOLBIAC BATTLE

A pivotal moment in Clovis's reign was his conversion to Christianity around 496 A.D. According to tradition, Clovis converted after praying to the Christian God for victory in battle. His baptism, along with that of 3,000 of his warriors, by Saint Remigius, the bishop of Reims, had profound implications. This conversion aligned the Frankish Kingdom with the Roman Catholic Church, gaining the support of the Gallo-Roman population and establishing a close relationship between the Frankish rulers and the Church.

Clovis continued to expand his kingdom, defeating the Visigoths at the Battle of Vouillé in 507 A.D. and annexing their territories in Aquitaine. By the time of his death in 511 A.D., Clovis had established a vast kingdom that encompassed much of modern-day France and parts of Germany.

The Merovingian dynasty, though powerful, was marked by internal strife and division. Upon Clovis's death, his kingdom was divided among his four sons, leading to a period of fragmentation and infighting. Despite these challenges, the Merovingians laid the groundwork for the future unification of Western Europe under the Carolingians.

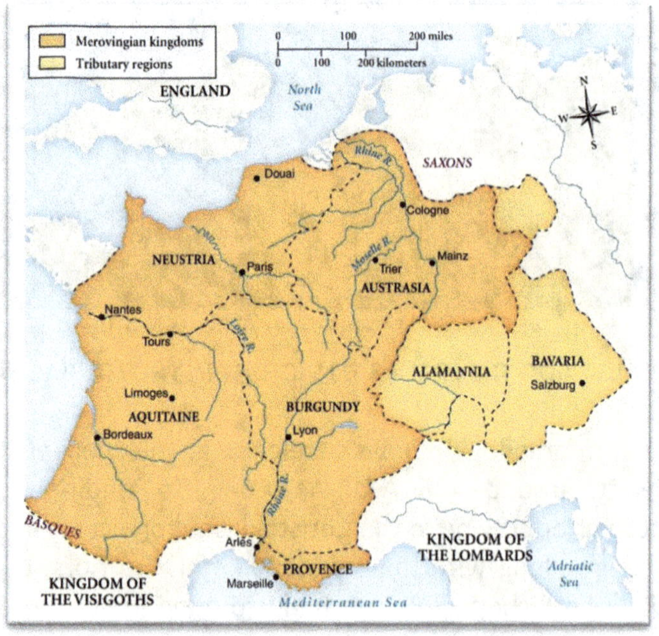

MAP OF THE MEROVINGIAN KINGDOMS

Charlemagne

The Carolingian dynasty, named after its most illustrious member, Charlemagne, succeeded the Merovingians and brought about a period of renewed stability and cultural flourishing in Western Europe.

Charlemagne, also known as Charles the Great, reigned from 768 to 814 A.D. He inherited the Frankish throne from his father, Pepin the Short, and his reign marked the pinnacle of Carolingian power. Charlemagne embarked on a series of military campaigns that expanded his empire to encompass much of Western and Central Europe, including modern-day France, Germany, Italy, and parts of Spain.

One of Charlemagne's most significant achievements was his coronation as Emperor of the Romans by Pope Leo III on Christmas Day in 800 A.D. This event symbolised the revival of the Western Roman Empire and established the precedent for the Holy Roman Empire, which would endure for centuries. Charlemagne's coronation also strengthened the alliance between the Frankish monarchy and the Papacy, reinforcing the notion of a united Christendom under a Christian emperor.

POPE LEO III CROWNING CHARLEMAGNE

Charlemagne's empire was characterised by its administrative and legal reforms, which sought to consolidate and govern the vast territories under his control. He appointed counts and bishops to administer local regions and established the Missi Dominici, royal agents who ensured compliance with imperial directives. These reforms enhanced the central authority and helped maintain order across the empire.

The Carolingian Renaissance was a period of cultural and intellectual revival initiated by Charlemagne. He established a palace school at Aachen (Aix-la-Chapelle) and invited scholars from across Europe, including Alcuin of York, to foster learning and scholarship. This renaissance saw the standardisation of Latin, the preservation and copying of classical texts, and advancements in art, architecture, and education. The development of the Carolingian minuscule, a clear and legible script, facilitated the dissemination of knowledge and became the basis for modern European handwriting.

THE PALACE SCHOOL AT AACHEN (AIX-LA-CHAPELLE) 792-805

Charlemagne also promoted Christianity throughout his empire, supporting the construction of churches and monasteries and encouraging missionary activities. His efforts to Christianise the Saxons, though often brutal, resulted in the integration of these peoples into his realm and the spread of Christianity in Northern Europe.

Despite his achievements, Charlemagne's empire faced challenges following his death in 814 A.D. His son, Louis the Pious, struggled to maintain the unity of the empire, and internal conflicts among his grandsons led to the Treaty of Verdun in 843 A.D. This treaty divided the Carolingian Empire into three distinct kingdoms, laying the groundwork for the future political landscape of Europe.

The Merovingian and Carolingian dynasties were instrumental in shaping the early medieval history of France and Western Europe. The rise of the Franks under Clovis established a powerful kingdom, while Charlemagne's reign marked a period of unification, cultural revival, and the creation of a legacy that would influence European history for centuries to come.

SUMMARY:

The Merovingian and Carolingian dynasties were instrumental in shaping the early medieval history of France and Western Europe. The rise of the Franks under Clovis established a powerful kingdom, while Charlemagne's reign marked a period of unification, cultural revival, and the creation of a legacy that would influence European history for centuries to come.

KEY PEOPLE, PLACES, AND EVENTS OF THE ERA

PEOPLE:

Clovis I (466-511) - Founder of the Merovingian dynasty and the first king to unite all Frankish tribes under one ruler.

Charlemagne (742-814) - The most famous Carolingian ruler, who expanded the Frankish kingdom into a vast empire and promoted a revival of learning and culture.

Louis the Pious (778-840) - Charlemagne's son who succeeded him and faced challenges in maintaining the empire's unity.

PLACES:

Paris - A significant political and cultural centre during both the Merovingian and Carolingian periods, eventually becoming the capital of France.

Aachen - Charlemagne's favoured residence and the centre of his empire, where he built his palace and the Palatine Chapel.

Tours - Known for the Battle of Tours (732), where Charles Martel, Charlemagne's grandfather, defeated the Moors, halting their advance into Europe.

EVENTS:

Conversion of Clovis to Christianity (496) - Clovis' conversion to Christianity, specifically Catholicism, played a crucial role in the Christianisation of Western Europe.

Division of the Carolingian Empire (843) - The Treaty of Verdun divided Charlemagne's empire among his grandsons, leading to the formation of West Francia (future France), East Francia (future Germany), and Middle Francia.

Viking Raids (8th-10th centuries) - The Carolingian Empire faced numerous Viking invasions, which disrupted trade and stability, contributing to the fragmentation of political authority.

CHAPTER 4

THE CAPETIAN AND MEDIEVAL FRANCE

987 - 1328

The Capetian dynasty began with the coronation of Hugh Capet in 987 A.D., marking the end of the Carolingian rule and the beginning of a new era for France. Hugh Capet, previously Duke of France and Count of Paris, was elected king by the French nobility, establishing a lineage that would rule France for over three centuries.

Initially, the early Capetian kings, including Hugh's successors Robert II, Henry I, and Philip I, controlled a relatively small domain centred around the Île-de-France. Their power was limited, as the kingdom was fragmented into territories ruled by powerful feudal lords who often wielded more influence than the king himself. However, the Capetians employed strategic marriages, alliances, and the gradual acquisition of land to strengthen their position.

Philip II Augustus (r. 1180-1223) was a pivotal figure in solidifying Capetian authority. He expanded the royal domain through conquest and diplomacy, most notably by reclaiming territories from the English crown. Philip's victory at the Battle of Bouvines in 1214 significantly enhanced the prestige and power of the French monarchy. By the end of his reign, the Capetians had transformed France into a centralised and cohesive kingdom.

THE CORONATION OF PHILIP II AUGUSTUS

Feudal Society

Medieval France under the Capetians was characterised by a feudal society where the king's authority was mediated through a hierarchy of lords and vassals. The social structure was divided into three main estates: the clergy, the nobility, and the peasantry.

The manorial system formed the economic backbone of feudal society. Lords owned large estates called manors, which were worked by peasants and serfs in exchange for protection and the right to work the land. The manorial system was self-sufficient, with manors producing most of what they needed for survival. Lords provided justice and protection, while peasants owed labour and a portion of their produce.

Chivalry was the code of conduct associated with the medieval knightly class. It emphasised virtues such as bravery, honour, and respect for women and the weak. Knights were expected to defend their lord's interests, fight in the king's wars, and participate in tournaments that displayed their martial skills. The ideal of chivalry was often romanticised in literature, as seen in the epic tales of Arthurian legend and the chansons de geste, such as "The Song of Roland."

THE EIGHT PHASES OF 'THE SONG OF ROLAND' ILLUSTRATED BY SIMON MARMION (15TH CENTURY)

The Crusades

France played a significant role in the Crusades, a series of religious wars sanctioned by the Church to reclaim the Holy Land from Muslim control. French knights and nobles were among the most enthusiastic participants, driven by religious fervour, the promise of land and wealth, and the opportunity to gain honour and prestige.

The First Crusade (1096-1099) saw notable French leaders, including Raymond IV of Toulouse and Godfrey of Bouillon, lead armies to the Holy Land. The Crusaders successfully captured Jerusalem in 1099, establishing several Crusader states.

MEDIEVAL MANUSCRIPT SHOWING THE SIEGE OF JERUSALEM (1099)

King Louis VII participated in the Second Crusade (1147-1149), which was less successful, marked by military setbacks and strategic failures. Despite these challenges, the Crusading spirit remained strong in France.

The Third Crusade (1189-1192) featured Philip II Augustus alongside Richard the Lionheart of England and Frederick Barbarossa of the Holy Roman Empire. Although Jerusalem was not recaptured, the Crusade achieved significant victories, including the capture of Acre.

The French continued to be involved in subsequent Crusades, with Saint Louis IX leading the Seventh and Eighth Crusades in the mid-13th century. Despite their efforts, the Crusaders ultimately failed to secure lasting control over the Holy Land, with the final fall of Acre in 1291 marking the end of the Crusader states.

The Hundred Years' War

Although extending slightly beyond the Capetian period, the Hundred Years' War was a defining conflict between England and France, rooted in territorial disputes and claims to the French throne. The war began in 1337 when Edward III of England asserted his claim to the French crown, challenging the Valois dynasty.

The war was characterised by several phases of intense military campaigns and periods of uneasy truce. Early English victories, such as the Battle of Crécy (1346) and the Battle of Poitiers (1356), demonstrated the effectiveness of English longbowmen and resulted in significant territorial gains for England.

The conflict reached a turning point with the arrival of Joan of Arc, a peasant girl who claimed to have received divine visions instructing her to support Charles VII, the rightful heir to the

French throne. Joan's leadership and inspiration were crucial in lifting the Siege of Orléans in 1429, a major turning point in the war. She also played a key role in the subsequent coronation of Charles VII at Reims.

JOAN OF ARC ENTERS ORLÉANS (1429)
PAINTING BY JEAN-JACQUES SCHERRER (1887)

Despite her capture and execution by the English in 1431, Joan of Arc became a martyr and a symbol of French national resistance. Her efforts revitalised French morale and contributed to a series of French victories that eventually led to the expulsion of English forces from most of French territory by 1453.

SUMMARY:

The Capetian dynasty and medieval France were marked by the establishment and consolidation of royal authority, the development of a feudal society, significant participation in the Crusades, and the prolonged conflict of the Hundred Years' War. These events and developments shaped the political, social, and cultural landscape of medieval France, leaving a lasting legacy on the nation's history.

PEOPLE:

Hugh Capet (987-996) - Founder of the Capetian dynasty, elected King of France in 987. His reign marked the beginning of the French monarchy's consolidation.

Robert II (996-1031) - Son of Hugh Capet, known as Robert the Pious. His reign saw the expansion of royal power and influence.

Philip I (1060-1108) - Known for conflicts with the Church and his excommunication over his marriage to Bertrade de Montfort.

Louis VI (1108-1137) - Strengthened royal power and increased control over rebellious nobles, earning the nickname "Louis the Fat."

Louis VII (1137-1180) - Participated in the Second Crusade and was married to Eleanor of Aquitaine before their marriage was annulled.

Philip II Augustus (1180-1223) - Expanded French territories significantly through wars and alliances, and played a key role in the Third Crusade.

Louis IX (1226-1270) -Known as Saint Louis, he was canonised for his piety and justice, and led the Seventh and Eighth Crusades.

Philip IV (1285-1314) - Known as Philip the Fair, he strengthened the monarchy and clashed with the Papacy, leading to the Avignon Papacy.

PLACES:

Paris - Capital city of France, political and cultural centre during the Capetian dynasty. Home to Notre-Dame Cathedral, whose construction began in 1163.

Reims - Site of the coronation of French kings, where the first Capetian king, Hugh Capet, was crowned.

Île-de-France - The core domain of the Capetian kings, a significant region that formed the power base for the monarchy.

Normandy - A powerful duchy in northern France, frequently contested between French and English crowns, notably during the reign of Philip II Augustus.

Avignon - Became the residence of the Papacy during the Avignon Papacy (1309-1377) initiated by conflicts with Philip IV.

EVENTS:

Coronation of Hugh Capet (987) - Marked the beginning of the Capetian dynasty, which would rule France for centuries.

Battle of Hastings (1066) - Although primarily an English event, the battle had significant repercussions for France, as William the Conqueror, Duke of Normandy, became King of England.

Second Crusade (1147-1149) - Louis VII's participation in this Crusade marked an important involvement of the French monarchy in Crusader efforts.

Battle of Bouvines (1214) - Philip II Augustus defeated an alliance of England, Flanders, and the Holy Roman Empire, solidifying his control over French territories.

Seventh Crusade (1248-1254) - Led by Louis IX, this Crusade ended in failure, with the king captured and later ransomed.

Treaty of Paris (1259) - Agreement between Louis IX of France and Henry III of England, settling territorial disputes and establishing clearer borders.

Conflict with the Papacy (1301-1303) - Philip IV's struggle with Pope Boniface VIII over taxation and authority led to the temporary relocation of the Papacy to Avignon.

Dissolution of the Knights Templar (1307) - Philip IV arrested and dissolved the Knights Templar, seizing their assets and reducing their influence.

CHAPTER 5

THE RENAISSANCE AND THE VALOIS DYNASTY

1328 - 1589

The Renaissance, a period of cultural rebirth and intellectual revival, began in Italy in the 14th century and gradually spread across Europe, reaching France in the early 16th century. The Valois kings, especially Francis I (r. 1515-1547), played a crucial role in fostering this cultural transformation.

Cultural Renaissance

Francis I was a great patron of the arts and a key figure in bringing the Renaissance to France. His reign saw the establishment of the Château de Chambord, an architectural masterpiece that blended Gothic and Renaissance styles, and the Château de Fontainebleau, where Italian artists such as Leonardo da Vinci were invited to work. Da Vinci spent the last years of his life in France under Francis I's patronage, bringing with him the famous painting 'Mona Lisa'.

The influence of the Italian Renaissance on France extended beyond architecture to literature, philosophy, and the sciences. The printing press, introduced in the late 15th century, facilitated the spread of Renaissance humanism. Prominent French humanists such as François Rabelais and Michel de Montaigne contributed significantly to Renaissance thought, promoting ideas of individualism, critical thinking, and the importance of education.

THE CHÂTEAU DE FONTAINEBLEAU

The French Renaissance also saw advancements in the visual arts. Artists like Jean Clouet and François Clouet produced detailed portraits that captured the likenesses and personalities of their subjects with remarkable accuracy. The era's emphasis on classical learning and aesthetic beauty had a lasting impact on French culture and education.

Religious Wars

The French Wars of Religion were a series of conflicts that erupted in the latter half of the 16th century, rooted in religious, political, and social tensions. These wars pitted the Catholics against the Huguenots (French Protestants), leading to decades of turmoil and violence.

The rise of Protestantism in France, influenced by the Reformation movements in Germany and Switzerland, led to significant religious division. The Huguenots, inspired by the teachings of John Calvin, gained substantial support among the French nobility and urban populations. This growing Protestant movement threatened the established Catholic order, leading to increasing hostility.

The conflict began in earnest in 1562 with the Massacre of Vassy, where a group of Huguenots were attacked by the troops of Francis, Duke of Guise. This event triggered a series of eight wars, marked by massacres, assassinations, and pitched battles. Notable incidents include the St. Bartholomew's Day Massacre in 1572, where thousands of Huguenots were killed in Paris and other cities, exacerbating the animosity between the two factions.

THE MASSACRE OF VASSY (1562)

The wars were not merely religious but also involved political power struggles, with various factions vying for control of the French crown. The Catherine de' Medici, the mother of three successive French kings (Francis II, Charles IX, and Henry III), played a complex and often controversial role, attempting to navigate and mediate the conflict through a combination of diplomacy and strategic marriages.

CATHERINE DE' MEDICI

Henry IV

The resolution of the religious wars came with the rise of Henry IV, a Huguenot who converted to Catholicism to secure his position as king and end the civil strife. Henry IV's famous declaration, "Paris is well worth a Mass," underscored his pragmatic approach to governance and his commitment to peace.

In 1598, Henry IV issued the Edict of Nantes, a landmark decree that granted substantial rights and freedoms to the Huguenots while reaffirming Catholicism as the state religion. The Edict provided for the freedom of worship, the right to hold public office, and the establishment of Protestant strongholds, effectively ending the religious wars and bringing a measure of religious tolerance to France.

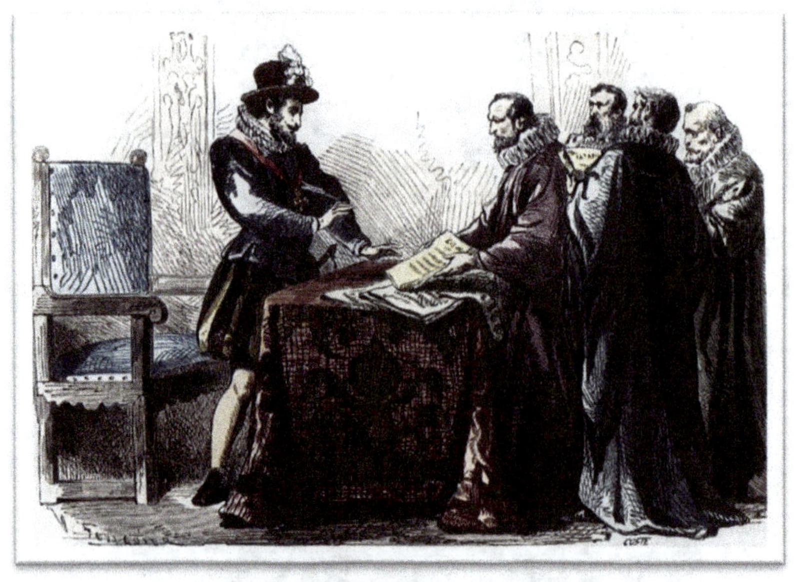

HENRY IV SIGNING THE EDICT OF NANTES

Henry IV's reign marked a period of recovery and rebuilding. He focused on economic reforms, infrastructure development, and strengthening the central authority of the monarchy. His efforts to restore peace and stability laid the foundation for the future prosperity of France.

SUMMARY:

The Renaissance and the Valois dynasty era were characterised by a profound cultural revival, significant religious conflict, and the eventual establishment of religious tolerance. The influence of the Italian Renaissance enriched French art, literature, and intellectual life, while the resolution of the French Wars of Religion under Henry IV paved the way for a more unified and peaceful France.

PEOPLE:

Philip VI (1328-1350) - First King of France from the Valois dynasty. His reign saw the beginning of the Hundred Years' War against England.

Charles V (1364-1380) - Known as Charles the Wise, he effectively reorganised the French military and administration during the Hundred Years' War.

Joan of Arc (1412-1431) - A peasant girl who led French forces to several important victories during the Hundred Years' War, leading to the coronation of Charles VII.

Charles VII (1422-1461) - Recovered France from English occupation with the help of Joan of Arc and implemented significant military reforms.

Louis XI (1461-1483) - Known as the "Universal Spider" for his complex web of political and diplomatic manoeuvres, he strengthened the central authority of the French monarchy.

Francis I (1515-1547) - A patron of the arts and a key figure in the French Renaissance. His reign saw significant cultural development and conflict with the Holy Roman Empire.

Henry II (1547-1559) - Continued his father Francis I's policies but died from injuries sustained in a jousting tournament, leading to instability.

Catherine de' Medici (1519-1589) - Queen consort of Henry II and influential regent for her sons. Known for her involvement in the French Wars of Religion.

Henry III (1574-1589) - Last Valois king of France, his reign was marked by the French Wars of Religion and political instability.

PLACES:

Paris - Continued to be the political and cultural centre of France, home to many significant events during the Valois dynasty.

Orléans - Site of a pivotal victory led by Joan of Arc in 1429, which turned the tide of the Hundred Years' War in favour of the French. Château de Chambord - A prime example of Renaissance architecture, built during the reign of Francis I.

Château de Fontainebleau - A royal residence that was significantly expanded by Francis I, reflecting the Renaissance style and housing many works of art.

Reims - Traditional site of the coronation of French kings, where Charles VII was crowned thanks to Joan of Arc's efforts.

Avignon - Home to the Papacy during the Avignon Papacy (1309-1377), its influence lingered into the Renaissance period.

EVENTS:

Beginning of the Hundred Years' War (1337) - A protracted conflict between England and France over territorial claims and the French crown, starting under Philip VI.

Battle of Crécy (1346) - A major battle during the Hundred Years' War where the English achieved a decisive victory over the French.

Battle of Agincourt (1415) - Another significant English victory during the Hundred Years' War, leading to English control over parts of France.

Siege of Orléans (1428-1429) - Marked a turning point in the Hundred Years' War with Joan of Arc's leadership leading to a crucial French victory.

Treaty of Arras (1435) - An agreement between Charles VII and Philip the Good, Duke of Burgundy, which ended their feud and strengthened France against England.

End of the Hundred Years' War (1453) - Marked by the French recapture of Bordeaux and other territories, solidifying French sovereignty.

Concordat of Bologna (1516) - An agreement between Francis I and Pope Leo X that allowed the French king to nominate bishops, strengthening royal control over the Church in France.

French Wars of Religion (1562-1598) - A series of conflicts between Catholics and Huguenots (Protestants) that profoundly affected French society and politics.

St. Bartholomew's Day Massacre (1572) - A violent clash in Paris where thousands of Huguenots were killed, exacerbating the French Wars of Religion.

Edict of Nantes (1598) - Issued by Henry IV (who succeeded the Valois dynasty), it granted religious tolerance to Huguenots and ended the French Wars of Religion.

CHAPTER 6

THE BOURBONS AND ABSOLUTE MONARCHY

1589 - 1792

The death of Henry IV in 1610 marked a turning point in French history. His assassination left the throne to his young son, Louis XIII, who was merely nine years old at the time. The regency was initially held by his mother, Marie de' Medici, but it was Cardinal Richelieu who would come to define the era.

Louis XIII and Cardinal Richelieu

Cardinal Richelieu (Armand Jean du Plessis) became the chief minister in 1624. His political acumen and determination transformed the nature of French governance. Richelieu's primary objective was the centralisation of power, reducing the influence of the nobility and ensuring the supremacy of the monarchy. He systematically dismantled the feudal power structures that had long fragmented France, replacing them with a more unified and controlled state.

CARDINAL RICHELIEU (ARMAND JEAN DU PLESSIS)

One of Richelieu's significant achievements was the suppression of the Huguenots, French Protestants who had previously enjoyed substantial political and military autonomy. The Siege of La Rochelle (1627-1628) was a pivotal moment, where Richelieu's forces captured the stronghold, leading to the Peace of Alais in 1629. This treaty curtailed the political and military privileges of the Huguenots while allowing them religious freedoms, thereby neutralising a significant threat to royal authority.

LA ROCHELLE DURING THE 1628 SIEGE

Richelieu also strengthened the administration by appointing intendants—royal officials tasked with enforcing central policies in the provinces. These intendants reported directly to the crown, bypassing the local nobility and further consolidating power within the monarchy.

Louis XIV

The reign of Louis XIV, also known as the Sun King, is often regarded as the epitome of absolute monarchy. Ascending to the throne in 1643 at the tender age of four, his early years were dominated by his mother, Anne of Austria, and her advisor, Cardinal Mazarin. The Fronde (1648-1653), a series of civil wars, revealed the fragility of royal power but also hardened young Louis's resolve to establish an unassailable monarchy.

Upon Mazarin's death in 1661, Louis XIV took direct control of the government, famously declaring, "L'État, c'est moi" ("I am the state"). His reign saw the further consolidation of royal power and the construction of an elaborate court at Versailles, a symbol of his absolute rule and the splendour of his reign.

LOUIS XIV (THE SUN KING)

Versailles was not merely a royal residence; it was a manifestation of Louis XIV's vision of absolute monarchy. The palace, with its opulent gardens and intricate architecture, became the centre of political power in France. By requiring the nobility to spend part of the year at Versailles, Louis ensured their loyalty and reduced their power in their own regions.

VERSAILLES PALACE GROUNDS

The Sun King's reign was marked by a series of wars aimed at expanding French territory and influence. These included the War of Devolution (1667-1668), the Franco-Dutch War (1672-1678), and the War of the Spanish Succession (1701-1714). While these conflicts initially brought territorial gains, they also strained the French economy and led to widespread suffering among the population.

Culturally, Louis XIV's reign was a golden age for France. He was a patron of the arts, supporting figures such as Molière, (Jean-Baptiste Poquelin), Jean Racine and Jean-Baptiste Lully, fostering the development of French classicism. The establishment of institutions like the Académie Française cemented France's cultural hegemony in Europe.

The Sun King's policy of Gallicanism asserted the independence of the French Church from papal authority, reinforcing his control over religious matters. However, his revocation of the Edict of Nantes in 1685, which had granted religious tolerance to the Huguenots, led to significant persecution and the emigration of many skilled Protestants, negatively impacting the French economy.

MOLIÈRE IN CLASSICAL DRESS

SUMMARY:

The period of Louis XIII and Louis XIV marked the high point of absolute monarchy in France. Through centralisation, cultural patronage, and the display of immense power, the Bourbons established a legacy of strong, centralised rule that would deeply influence the subsequent history of France, even as it sowed the seeds for future discontent and revolution.

KEY PEOPLE, PLACES, AND EVENTS OF THE ERA

Henry IV (1589-1610) - First Bourbon king of France. Known for issuing the Edict of Nantes in 1598, which granted religious tolerance to Huguenots, and for stabilising and revitalising France after the Wars of Religion.

Cardinal Richelieu (1585-1642) - Chief minister to Louis XIII. Strengthened royal authority, suppressed noble power, and laid the groundwork for absolute monarchy.

Louis XIII (1610-1643) - King of France who worked with Cardinal Richelieu to centralise power and diminish the influence of the nobility.

Louis XIV (1643-1715) - Known as the Sun King, he epitomised absolute monarchy. His reign saw the expansion of French influence in Europe and the construction of the Palace of Versailles.

Jean-Baptiste Colbert (1619-1683) - Finance minister under Louis XIV, who implemented economic reforms to strengthen the French economy through mercantilism.

Louis XV (1715-1774) - His reign was marked by economic troubles and a series of military conflicts that weakened France's position in Europe.

Madame de Pompadour (1721-1764) - Influential mistress of Louis XV who played a key role in French politics, culture, and art.

Louis XVI (1774-1792) - Last Bourbon king before the French Revolution. His attempts at reform were thwarted by deep-seated financial problems and political opposition, leading to his execution during the Revolution.

Marie Antoinette (1755-1793) - Queen consort of Louis XVI, known for her extravagant lifestyle. She became a symbol of the excesses of the monarchy and was executed during the Revolution.

Versailles - The royal palace and centre of political power under Louis XIV. Symbol of absolute monarchy and opulence.

Paris - Continued to be the political, economic, and cultural heart of France, playing a crucial role during the Revolution.

Fontainebleau - Another royal residence, used frequently by Louis XIII and Louis XIV for hunting and political gatherings.

Rocroi - Site of the Battle of Rocroi (1643), a significant French victory in the Thirty Years' War under Louis XIII's reign.

La Rochelle - A Huguenot stronghold besieged and captured by Cardinal Richelieu in 1628, which significantly weakened Protestant power in France.

Nantes - Site where the Edict of Nantes was issued in 1598, promoting religious tolerance, and later where it was revoked by Louis XIV in 1685.

EVENTS:

Edict of Nantes (1598) - Issued by Henry IV to grant religious freedom to Huguenots, ending the French Wars of Religion.

Siege of La Rochelle (1627-1628) - Cardinal Richelieu's victory over the Huguenots, strengthening royal control and diminishing Protestant influence.

Thirty Years' War (1618-1648) - A European conflict involving France under Louis XIII and Cardinal Richelieu, which ended with the Peace of Westphalia and increased French influence.

Construction of Versailles (1661-1682) - Begun under Louis XIV, this symbol of absolute monarchy became the political and cultural centre of France.

Revocation of the Edict of Nantes (1685) - Louis XIV's decision to revoke religious tolerance, leading to persecution of Huguenots and significant emigration.

War of the Spanish Succession (1701-1714) - A major European conflict in which France, under Louis XIV, fought to place his grandson on the Spanish throne, ultimately resulting in the Treaty of Utrecht.

Seven Years' War (1756-1763) - A global conflict involving France, which suffered significant territorial losses, including Canada to Britain.

Louis XVI's Reign (1774-1792) - Marked by financial crisis, attempts at reform, and escalating tensions leading to the French Revolution.

French Revolution (1789-1792) - A period of radical social and political upheaval that ended absolute monarchy and led to the establishment of the French Republic. Key events include the Storming of the Bastille (1789) and the execution of Louis XVI (1793).

Execution of Louis XVI (1793) - Louis XVI was executed by guillotine, marking the end of the Bourbon monarchy and the rise of revolutionary France.

CHAPTER 7

THE AGE OF REVOLUTION AND NAPOLEON

1789-1815

The Enlightenment, an intellectual and philosophical movement that dominated the 18th century, laid the groundwork for the transformative events that followed. Thinkers such as Voltaire (François Arouet), Jean Jacques Rousseau, and Charles Montesquieu challenged traditional doctrines and advocated for reason, science, and individual rights. This period, also known as the Age of Reason, saw the proliferation of ideas that questioned absolute monarchy, the privileges of the nobility and clergy, and the inefficacies of traditional governance.

The Enlightenment

Voltaire's critique of the Church and advocacy for freedom of speech, Rousseau's ideas on direct democracy and the social contract, and Montesquieu's theory of the separation of powers profoundly influenced the intellectual landscape of Europe. The Encyclopédie, edited by Denis Diderot and Jean le Rond d'Alembert, disseminated Enlightenment ideas widely, encouraging critical thinking and the pursuit of knowledge.

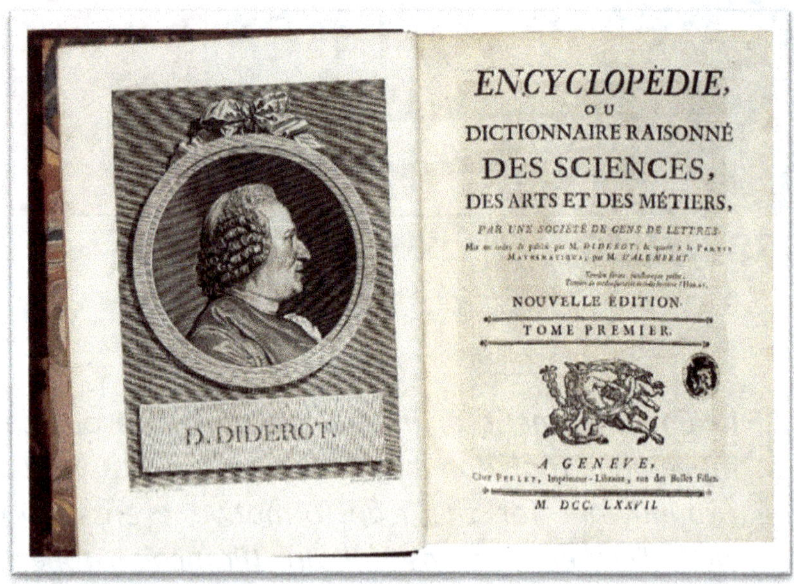

THE ENCYCLOPÉDIE OF THE SCIENCES, ARTS, AND CRAFTS

The salons of Paris, where intellectuals gathered to discuss and debate, played a crucial role in spreading these ideas. The Enlightenment fostered an environment of scepticism towards traditional authorities and inspired the revolutionary zeal that would soon erupt in France. The emphasis on equality, liberty, and fraternity resonated deeply with an increasingly literate and aware populace, setting the stage for the revolutionary upheaval to come.

The French Revolution

The French Revolution began in 1789, catalysed by economic distress, social inequality, and a burgeoning desire for political reform. The financial crisis, exacerbated by France's involvement in the American War of Independence, forced Louis XVI to convene the Estates-General in May 1789, the first time since 1614. This assembly, meant to address fiscal issues, quickly became a platform for broader demands for change.

The Tennis Court Oath in June 1789 marked the determination of the Third Estate to draft a new constitution, leading to the formation of the National Assembly. The storming of the Bastille on 14 July 1789 became a symbol of revolutionary fervour and the collapse of royal authority. The revolutionaries sought to dismantle the old regime, abolishing feudal privileges and issuing the Declaration of the Rights of Man and of the Citizen, which enshrined principles of liberty, equality, and fraternity.

MAXIMILIEN ROBESPIERRE LED THE 'REIGN OF TERROR'

However, the revolution soon took a more radical turn. The Reign of Terror (1793-1794), led by Maximilien Robespierre and the Committee of Public Safety, sought to protect the revolution from internal and external enemies. Thousands were executed by guillotine, including King Louis XVI who was found guilty of treason and executed at the guillotine on 21 January 1793. Marie Antoinette was executed nine months later. The radical phase aimed to establish a republic of virtue but ultimately descended into paranoia and violence, ending with Robespierre's own execution in July 1794.

KING LOUIS XVI EXECUTED ON 21ST JANUARY 1793

The Thermidorian Reaction brought a more conservative phase, culminating in the establishment of the Directory in 1795. Yet, the Directory was marred by corruption and inefficiency, unable to address the ongoing economic and social crises.

Amidst this turmoil, Napoleon Bonaparte rose to prominence. A successful military leader, Napoleon seized power through a coup d'état in 1799, establishing the Consulate with himself as First Consul. This marked the end of the revolutionary decade and the beginning of a new era.

Napoleon Bonaparte

Napoleon Bonaparte's ascendancy significantly transformed France and reshaped the political landscape of Europe. In 1804, he crowned himself Emperor, initiating a series of military campaigns known as the Napoleonic Wars, which spanned from 1803 to 1815. His conquests and military strategies redrew the map of Europe, spreading revolutionary principles and systematically dismantling feudal structures across the continent.

Domestically, Napoleon implemented a series of profound administrative reforms that had long-lasting effects. The introduction of the Napoleonic Code in 1804 codified a uniform set of laws that emphasised equality before the law, religious tolerance, and merit-based advancement. This legal framework significantly influenced many modern legal systems and remains a cornerstone of French civil law to this day.

In addition to legal reforms, Napoleon restructured the education system, established the Bank of France to stabilize the economy, and streamlined the bureaucracy to create a more efficient state apparatus. His Concordat of 1801 with the Catholic Church aimed to restore stability to church-state relations, although the state retained significant control over religious matters, balancing power between secular and religious authorities.

EMPEROR NAPOLEON BONAPARTE (1803)

Despite his numerous successes, Napoleon's relentless ambition eventually led to his overreach. The disastrous invasion of Russia in 1812 marked the beginning of his downfall, as the harsh winter and logistical failures decimated his Grande Armée. This catastrophic failure emboldened his enemies, leading to the formation of the Sixth Coalition. The coalition, comprising major European powers, decisively defeated Napoleon at the Battle of Leipzig in 1813.

In 1814, facing invasion and insurmountable opposition, Napoleon abdicated the throne and was exiled to the island of Elba. His dramatic return to power in 1815, known as the Hundred Days, ended with his final defeat at the Battle of Waterloo on 18 June 1815. Following this defeat, Napoleon was exiled to the remote island of Saint Helena, where he spent the remaining years of his life, reflecting on his legacy and the empire he had built and lost.

NAPOLEON'S DEFEAT AT THE BATTLE OF LEIPZIG IN 1813

SUMMARY:

The Napoleonic era profoundly reshaped Europe, ending the revolutionary period and ushering in a century of conservative reaction but also sowing the seeds for future nationalist and liberal movements. The legacy of the Enlightenment and the revolution, coupled with Napoleon's reforms, left an indelible mark on the course of European history.

PEOPLE:

Louis XVI (1754-1793) - The last king of France before the fall of the monarchy during the French Revolution. Executed by guillotine in 1793.

Maximilien Robespierre (1758-1794) - Influential leader during the French Revolution, key figure in the Reign of Terror, and member of the Committee of Public Safety.

Jean-Paul Marat (1743-1793) - Radical journalist and politician, whose assassination made him a martyr for the revolutionary cause.

Georges Danton (1759-1794) - Leading figure in the early stages of the French Revolution and first president of the Committee of Public Safety.

Napoleon Bonaparte (1769-1821) - Military general who rose to power during the French Revolution, eventually becoming Emperor of the French. His conquests and reforms had a lasting impact on France and Europe.

Josephine de Beauharnais (1763-1814) - First wife of Napoleon Bonaparte and Empress of the French. Played a significant role in Napoleon's rise.

Horatio Nelson (1758-1805) - British admiral known for his victories against Napoleon's navy, including the Battle of Trafalgar in 1805 where he lost his life.

Alexander I of Russia (1777-1825) - Emperor of Russia, initially an ally then a key opponent of Napoleon, playing a major role in his defeat.

PLACES:

Paris - Epicentre of the French Revolution, where significant events such as the Storming of the Bastille and the Reign of Terror took place.

Versailles - Royal palace and symbol of monarchical opulence, where the Estates-General was convened in 1789, leading to the Revolution.

Bastille - Fortress in Paris whose storming on 14 July 1789 marked the beginning of the French Revolution.

Tuileries Palace - Royal residence in Paris, stormed by revolutionaries in 1792, leading to the imprisonment of Louis XVI and his family.

Waterloo - Site in Belgium of Napoleon's final defeat by the Seventh Coalition, The Battle of Waterloo in 1815 marked the end of the Napoleonic Wars.

Austerlitz - Location in present-day Czech Republic of Napoleon's greatest victory in 1805, defeating the Russian and Austrian armies.

Leipzig - Site of the Battle of Leipzig (1813), also known as the Battle of Nations, where Napoleon faced a decisive defeat by the coalition forces.

EVENTS:

Storming of the Bastille (14 July 1789) - A symbolic act of revolution against the monarchy, marking the beginning of widespread uprisings.

Declaration of the Rights of Man and of the Citizen (1789) - A fundamental document of the French Revolution, proclaiming the equality and rights of all male citizens.

Reign of Terror (1793-1794) - A period of extreme political repression led by the Committee of Public Safety, resulting in mass executions.

Execution of Louis XVI (1793) - The former king was executed by guillotine, symbolising the end of the monarchy.

Coup of 18 Brumaire (1799) - Napoleon's seizure of power, overthrowing the Directory and establishing the Consulate.

Napoleonic Code (1804) - A comprehensive set of civil laws established by Napoleon, forming the basis for many modern legal systems.

Coronation of Napoleon (1804) - Napoleon crowned himself Emperor of the French, marking the transition from republic to empire.

Battle of Austerlitz (1805) - Napoleon's decisive victory over Russian and Austrian forces, establishing his dominance in Europe.

Battle of Trafalgar (1805) - Naval battle in which the British fleet, led by Admiral Nelson, defeated Napoleon's navy, ensuring British naval supremacy.

Peninsular War (1808-1814) - A conflict in Spain and Portugal where Spanish, Portuguese, and British forces fought against French occupation.

Russian Campaign (1812) - Napoleon's disastrous invasion of Russia, leading to a significant loss of French troops and weakening of his empire.

Battle of Leipzig (1813) - Also known as the Battle of Nations, where Napoleon faced a decisive defeat by the coalition forces of Austria, Prussia, Russia, and Sweden.

Exile to Elba (1814) - Napoleon was exiled to the island of Elba after his initial abdication, but he escaped in 1815, returning to power for the Hundred Days.

Battle of Waterloo (1815) - Napoleon's final defeat by the Seventh Coalition, leading to his second abdication and exile to Saint Helena.

Congress of Vienna (1814-1815) - A conference of European powers to reorganise Europe after the Napoleonic Wars, leading to a reshaped political map and balance of power.

CHAPTER 8

THE 19ᵀᴴ CENTURY – RESTORATION TO REPUBLIC

1815 - 1870

The fall of Napoleon Bonaparte in 1815 heralded the return of the Bourbon monarchy under Louis XVIII. This period, known as the Bourbon Restoration, aimed to reconcile revolutionary changes with the traditional monarchy. Louis XVIII, conscious of the volatile political climate, adopted a relatively moderate stance, issuing the Charter of 1814. This constitutional document retained many revolutionary and Napoleonic reforms, such as civil equality and the Napoleonic Code, while re-establishing the monarchy and maintaining a bicameral legislature.

Bourbon Restoration

The restoration was marked by political tensions. The Ultra-royalists, who sought a return to pre-revolutionary absolutism, clashed with liberals advocating for more democratic reforms. The assassination of the Duke of Berry in 1820, a potential heir to the throne, intensified these conflicts, leading to increased repression under the reign of Charles X, who succeeded Louis XVIII in 1824.

RETURN OF THE BOURBON MONARCHY UNDER LOUIS XVIII

Charles X's reactionary policies, including compensation for émigrés and the reintroduction of censorship, alienated much of the population. His July Ordinances of 1830, which dissolved the Chamber of Deputies and restricted the press, triggered the July Revolution. This uprising forced Charles X to abdicate, ending the Bourbon Restoration.

The July Monarchy

The July Revolution of 1830 brought Louis-Philippe, the "Citizen King," to the throne. Representing the Orléanist branch of the Bourbons, Louis-Philippe's reign is known as the July Monarchy. His ascent marked a shift from aristocratic to bourgeois dominance in French politics. The new regime adopted a more liberal constitution, the Charter of 1830, which reduced the king's powers and increased the influence of the legislative bodies.

A SCENE FROM THE JULY REVOLUTION OF 1830

Louis-Philippe's reign saw significant social and economic changes. The rise of the bourgeoisie was accompanied by rapid industrialisation. The expansion of railways, the growth of factories, and urbanisation transformed the French economy and society. However, the benefits of these changes were unevenly distributed, leading to social unrest.

Political tensions persisted as the working classes, disenfranchised by the property-based voting system, demanded more political rights. This discontent culminated in the Revolution of 1848, which was part of a wider wave of European revolutions. Louis-Philippe abdicated and fled to England, ending the July Monarchy.

LOUIS-PHILIPPE (THE "CITIZEN KING")

The Second Republic and Second Empire

The Revolution of 1848 led to the establishment of the Second Republic. Universal male suffrage was introduced, and the new republic adopted a progressive constitution. However, the republic faced significant challenges, including economic crises and political divisions between moderates and radicals.

Louis-Napoleon Bonaparte, nephew of Napoleon I, capitalised on these divisions. Elected President of the Republic in December 1848, he initially presented himself as a defender of the republic. However, in 1851, he staged a coup d'état, dissolving the National Assembly and later proclaiming himself Emperor Napoleon III, thus inaugurating the Second Empire in 1852.

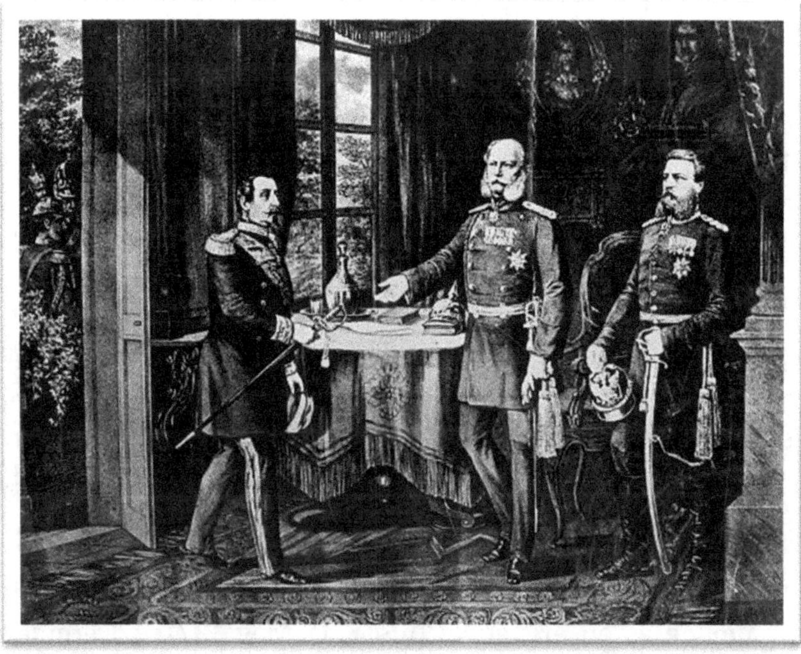

NAPOLEON III SURRENDERS TO WILHELM I AND CROWN PRINCE FREDERICK

Napoleon III's reign was characterised by authoritarian rule coupled with modernisation efforts. His government pursued extensive public works projects, including the renovation of Paris by Georges-Eugène Haussmann (commonly known as Baron Haussmann), which transformed the city with wide boulevards, parks, and modern infrastructure. Industrialisation continued to advance, fostering economic growth and development.

The Second Empire also pursued an ambitious foreign policy. Initially successful, exemplified by victories in the Crimean War and the Italian unification process, Napoleon III's regime eventually faced setbacks. The disastrous Franco-Prussian War (1870-1871) culminated in Napoleon III's capture and the collapse of the Second Empire.

The Paris Commune

Following France's defeat in the Franco-Prussian War, the collapse of the Second Empire led to the proclamation of the Third Republic. However, the aftermath of the war and the siege of Paris created severe hardships and political turmoil. In March 1871, radical socialists and workers in Paris, frustrated with the conservative government, established the Paris Commune.

The Commune represented a radical experiment in self-governance and socialism. It implemented progressive measures such as the separation of church and state, free education, and workers' control of enterprises. However, internal divisions and external threats plagued the Commune from the start.

The national government, based in Versailles, viewed the Commune as an existential threat. In May 1871, government troops launched a brutal assault on Paris, culminating in the "Semaine Sanglante" (Bloody Week), during which thousands of Communards were killed or executed.

A BARRICADE IN THE PARIS COMMUNE, MARCH 18, 1871

The fall of the Paris Commune marked a significant moment in French history. It highlighted the deep social and political divisions within France and left a lasting legacy in the collective memory of the French left. The suppression of the Commune consolidated the Third Republic, which would endure until the establishment of the Vichy regime in 1940.

SUMMARY:

The 19th century in France was a period of profound transformation, marked by the oscillation between monarchy and republic, the rise of the bourgeoisie, rapid industrialisation, and significant social upheavals. The legacies of these tumultuous decades would shape the future trajectory of France well into the 20th century.

KEY PEOPLE, PLACES, AND EVENTS OF THE ERA

PEOPLE

Louis XVIII (1814-1824) - Restored Bourbon king of France after the fall of Napoleon, attempted to balance between revolutionary ideals and monarchical tradition.

Charles X (1824-1830) - Younger brother of Louis XVIII, his reactionary policies led to the July Revolution of 1830 and his subsequent abdication.

Louis-Philippe I (1830-1848) - Known as the "Citizen King," he ascended the throne after the July Revolution, promoting liberal policies before being overthrown in the 1848 Revolution.

Napoleon III (1852-1870) - Nephew of Napoleon Bonaparte, he became President of the Second Republic and later Emperor of the Second French Empire, modernising France and leading it into the Franco-Prussian War.

Adolphe Thiers (1797-1877) - Historian, statesman, and key figure in the July Monarchy, he played a significant role in the establishment of the Third Republic.

Victor Hugo (1802-1885) - Renowned writer and political figure, whose works like "Les Misérables" and "The Hunchback of Notre-Dame" captured the social issues of his time.

Georges-Eugène Haussmann (1809-1891) - Appointed by Napoleon III, he oversaw the extensive urban renewal of Paris, transforming it into a modern city.

PLACES:

Paris - The centre of political, social, and cultural changes, witnessing revolutions, urban renewal, and becoming a symbol of modernisation.

Versailles - The location of significant political events, including the declaration of the Second Empire by Napoleon III.

Algiers - Capital of French Algeria, reflecting France's colonial expansion during the 19th century.

Metz - A strategic city in northeastern France, pivotal in the Franco-Prussian War.

Sedan - Site of the Battle of Sedan (1870), where Napoleon III was captured, leading to the collapse of the Second Empire.

EVENTS:

Congress of Vienna (1814-1815) - Aimed to restore pre-Napoleonic order in Europe, significantly impacting France's political landscape.

July Revolution (1830) - Overthrew Charles X, leading to the establishment of the July Monarchy under Louis-Philippe.

Revolution of 1848 - A series of revolutionary uprisings across Europe that led to the fall of Louis-Philippe and the establishment of the Second Republic in France.

Establishment of the Second Republic (1848) - Proclaimed after the 1848 Revolution, with Louis-Napoleon Bonaparte elected as its first President.

Coup d'état of 1851 - Led by Louis-Napoleon Bonaparte, dissolving the National Assembly and eventually establishing the Second Empire.

Crimean War (1853-1856) - France, under Napoleon III, allied with Britain and the Ottoman Empire against Russia, influencing European power dynamics.

Paris Renovation (1853-1870) - Major urban renewal project led by Haussmann, transforming Paris with wide boulevards, parks, and modern infrastructure.

Franco-Prussian War (1870-1871) - Conflict between France and Prussia, leading to the defeat of France, the fall of the Second Empire, and the unification of Germany.

Battle of Sedan (1870) - Decisive battle where Napoleon III was captured, marking the end of the Second Empire.

Proclamation of the Third Republic (1870) - Following the defeat in the Franco-Prussian War and the fall of Napoleon III, the Third Republic was established, marking a shift towards republicanism in France.

THE THIRD REPUBLIC AND WORLD WARS

1870 - 1945

The Belle Époque (Beautiful Era) was a period of relative peace and prosperity in France, lasting from the end of the Franco-Prussian War in 1871 until the outbreak of World War I in 1914. This era was marked by remarkable cultural, technological, and social advancements, fostering a sense of optimism and modernity.

The Belle Époque:

Paris, often referred to as the "City of Light," became the epicentre of artistic and intellectual life. The Eiffel Tower, completed in 1889 for the Exposition Universelle, symbolised the era's technological prowess and architectural innovation. The development of impressionism in painting, led by artists such as Claude Monet, Pierre-Auguste Renoir, and Edgar Degas, revolutionised the art world with its emphasis on light, colour, and everyday scenes.

THE EIFFEL TOWER COMPLETED IN 1889

In literature, the works of Émile Zola, Marcel Proust, and Victor Hugo explored social issues and human consciousness, while the theatre saw the rise of naturalism and symbolism. The Moulin Rouge and other cabarets became cultural landmarks, celebrating the era's joie de vivre.

PAINTING BY CLAUDE MONET 'SPRINGTIME'

Technological advancements flourished, with the advent of the automobile, the aeroplane, and innovations in telecommunications. The Paris Métro, inaugurated in 1900, exemplified the era's urban modernisation.

However, the Belle Époque also witnessed significant social tensions. One major event was the Dreyfus Affair, spanning from 1894 to 1906, which involved the wrongful conviction of Alfred Dreyfus, a Jewish army officer, for treason. This scandal, driven by anti-Semitic sentiments, exposed deep divisions in French society, highlighting issues of anti-Semitism, militarism, and injustice.

The nation split into Dreyfusards, who supported Dreyfus's innocence, and anti-Dreyfusards, who upheld his guilt. Intellectuals like Émile Zola played key roles, with Zola's

"J'Accuse...!" letter accusing the government of a cover-up, further intensifying the debate. The affair underscored the fragility of the Republic and left a lasting impact on French society.

ALFRED DREYFUS IN CAPTIVITY ON DEVIL'S ISLAND 1898

World War I

World War I, also known as the Great War, profoundly impacted France. The nation entered the war in August 1914 as part of the Allied Powers, facing the Central Powers led by Germany. The Western Front, which ran through northern and eastern France, became the primary theatre of conflict.

Trench warfare characterised the brutal and stagnant nature of the war. Battles such as the Battle of Verdun (1916) and the Battle of the Somme (1916) resulted in enormous casualties and destruction. The French military, led by figures such as Marshal Philippe Pétain and General Ferdinand Foch, endured immense hardships but played a crucial role in repelling German advances.

GERMAN SOLDIERS IN THE TRENCHES, JULY 1916

The war had a profound social and economic impact on France. Millions of soldiers and civilians were killed or wounded, and the country suffered extensive damage to its infrastructure and landscapes. The war effort also led to significant changes in French society, including the mobilisation of women in the workforce and increased state intervention in the economy.

The Armistice of 11 November 1918 ended the fighting, and the subsequent Treaty of Versailles (1919) imposed severe penalties on Germany. While the treaty aimed to ensure lasting peace, it also sowed the seeds of future conflict. The war left France deeply scarred, both physically and psychologically, and the memory of the Great War would profoundly shape the interwar period and beyond.

Interwar Period

The interwar period in France was marked by political instability and social change. The Third Republic faced numerous challenges, including economic difficulties, political fragmentation, and the rise of extremist movements.

The Great Depression of the 1930s exacerbated economic woes, leading to widespread unemployment and social unrest. Political life was characterised by frequent changes in government and the emergence of polarised political forces. The Popular Front, a coalition of left-wing parties led by Léon Blum, briefly came to power in 1936, implementing social reforms such as the 40-hour workweek and paid holidays. However, the government struggled to address the broader economic crisis and was ultimately short-lived.

SUFFERING AND WOES OF THE GREAT DEPRESSION 1930S

Culturally, the interwar period saw significant developments. The Surrealist movement, led by André Breton, Salvador Dalí, and others, pushed the boundaries of artistic and literary expression. Paris remained a hub for international artists and intellectuals, including Ernest Hemingway, F. Scott Fitzgerald, and Pablo Picasso.

Technological innovations continued, with advances in cinema, aviation, and radio transforming daily life. The spirit of modernism influenced architecture and design, exemplified by the works of Charles-Édouard Jeanneret better known as Le Corbusier and the Art Deco movement.

LE CORBUSIER SYNONYMOUS WITH THE 'ART DECO' MOVEMENT

Despite these cultural flourishes, the looming threat of fascism and the rising tensions in Europe cast a shadow over France. The country faced increasing political polarisation and was unprepared for the approaching storm of another world war.

World War II

World War II began in September 1939, and France quickly became a central battleground. The German Blitzkrieg campaign in May 1940 overwhelmed French defences, leading to the swift fall of France. By June 1940, German forces occupied Paris, and the French government, led by Marshal Philippe Pétain, signed an armistice, resulting in the establishment of Vichy France.

GERMAN SOLDIERS ON THE CHAMPS ÉLYSÉES ON 14 JUNE 1940

Vichy France, based in the unoccupied southern part of the country, collaborated with Nazi Germany, implementing authoritarian policies and participating in the persecution of Jews and other minorities. Pétain's regime aimed to restore traditional values, but its collaborationist stance and repression alienated many French citizens.

Amidst the occupation, the French Resistance emerged as a vital force against the Nazis and the Vichy regime. Led by figures such as Charles de Gaulle, who rallied Free French forces from exile in London, the resistance conducted sabotage, intelligence gathering, and guerrilla warfare. The Maquis, rural guerrilla bands, played a crucial role in harassing German forces and aiding Allied operations.

The turning point came with the D-Day landings on 6 June 1944, when Allied forces launched a massive invasion of Normandy. The liberation of Paris followed in August 1944, with de Gaulle leading a triumphant march down the Champs-Élysées. By May 1945, Germany had surrendered, marking the end of the war in Europe.

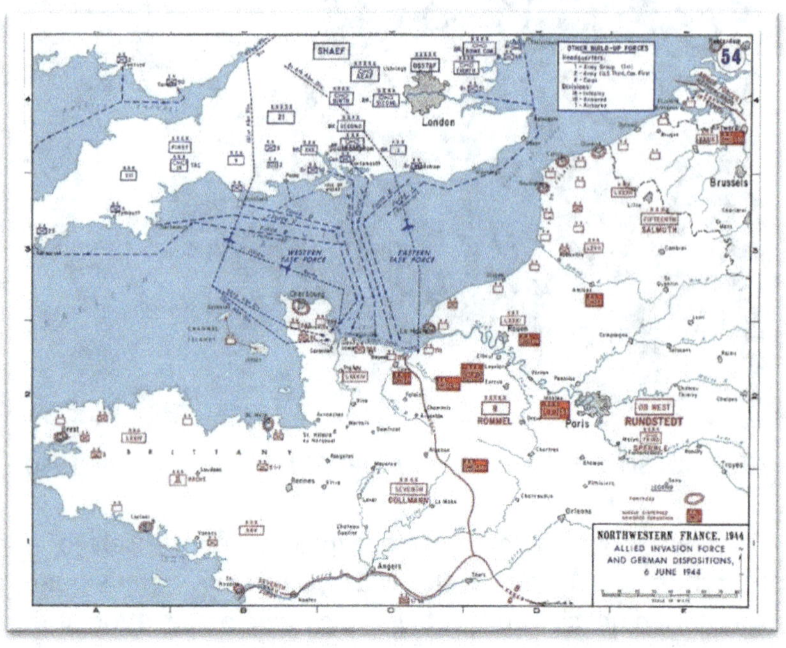

ALLIED INVASION PLANS AND GERMAN POSITIONS FOR THE INVASION OF NORMANDY

The war left France devastated, with significant loss of life, widespread destruction, and a deeply scarred national psyche. The post-war period would see the country grappling with reconstruction, political realignment, and the challenge of rebuilding its place in a rapidly changing world.

SUMMARY:

The 19th and early 20th centuries were transformative for France, encompassing periods of cultural flourishing, political upheaval, and profound social change. The legacies of the Belle Époque, the trauma of two world wars, and the resilience of the French people during times of occupation and resistance have indelibly shaped the nation's history and identity.

PEOPLE:

Adolphe Thiers (1797-1877) - First President of the Third Republic, instrumental in suppressing the Paris Commune and stabilising the new republic.

Georges Clemenceau (1841-1929) - Known as "The Tiger," he was a key figure during World War I, serving as Prime Minister and playing a major role in the Treaty of Versailles.

Ferdinand Foch (1851-1929) - Supreme Allied Commander during World War I, instrumental in leading the Allies to victory.

Philippe Pétain (1856-1951) - Celebrated as a hero of Verdun in World War I, later became the head of the Vichy government collaborating with Nazi Germany during World War II.

Charles de Gaulle (1890-1970) - Leader of the Free French Forces during World War II, later became President of France, leading the country through its post-war recovery.

Jean Jaurès (1859-1914) - Influential socialist leader and pacifist, assassinated on the eve of World War I.

Marie Curie (1867-1934) - Renowned scientist who won Nobel Prizes in Physics and Chemistry, contributing significantly to the field of radioactivity.

PLACES

Paris - Centre of political, cultural, and social life, playing a pivotal role in events like the Paris Commune, both World Wars, and the Liberation of Paris.

Versailles - Location of the signing of the Treaty of Versailles in 1919, which officially ended World War I.

Verdun - Site of one of the longest and bloodiest battles of World War I, symbolising French resilience and sacrifice.

Vichy - Capital of the Vichy government, which collaborated with Nazi Germany during World War II.

Normandy - Site of the D-Day landings on June 6, 1944, marking the beginning of the liberation of France during World War II.
Dunkirk - Location of the dramatic evacuation of Allied troops in 1940 during World War II.

EVENTS

Paris Commune (1871) - Radical socialist and revolutionary government that briefly ruled Paris before being violently suppressed.

Dreyfus Affair (1894-1906) - Political scandal involving the wrongful conviction of Jewish officer Alfred Dreyfus, highlighting deep divisions in French society over anti-Semitism and injustice.

World War I (1914-1918) - A global conflict in which France played a major role, enduring immense human and material losses, and emerging as one of the victorious Allied powers.

Battle of the Marne (1914) - A significant early battle in World War I where French and British forces halted the German advance, saving Paris from capture.

Treaty of Versailles (1919) - Peace treaty that ended World War I, imposing heavy reparations and territorial losses on Germany, significantly shaping the interwar period.

Great Depression (1929) - Worldwide economic downturn that severely impacted France, leading to political instability and social unrest.

Rise of the Popular Front (1936) - A coalition of left-wing parties that came to power in France, implementing social and labour reforms during a period of economic crisis.

Fall of France (1940) - Germany's invasion and swift defeat of French forces in World War II, leading to the occupation of France and the establishment of the Vichy regime.

Vichy Regime (1940-1944) - The authoritarian government led by Philippe Pétain, which collaborated with Nazi Germany during the occupation.

D-Day (1944) - Allied invasion of Normandy, marking the beginning of the liberation of France from Nazi occupation during World War II.

Liberation of Paris (1944) - The city was liberated by French and Allied forces in August 1944, marking a significant turning point in the liberation of France.

End of World War II (1945) - The defeat of Nazi Germany, leading to the restoration of the French Republic and the beginning of post-war reconstruction.

CHAPTER 10

POST-WAR FRANCE AND THE FIFTH REPUBLIC

1945 - 1981

The end of World War II marked the beginning of a significant period of reconstruction and modernisation in France. The nation, devastated by the war, faced the immense task of rebuilding its infrastructure, economy, and social fabric. The immediate post-war period saw the establishment of the Fourth Republic (1946-1958), which aimed to address these challenges.

Reconstruction

Economic Recovery was spurred by the Marshall Plan, through which the United States provided financial aid to help rebuild European economies. This aid, combined with national efforts, facilitated the recovery of industry and agriculture. Key sectors such as steel, coal, and manufacturing experienced significant growth, laying the foundations for modernisation.

France's post-war economic strategy focused on modernisation and state intervention. The establishment of national planning bodies like the Commissariat général du Plan under Jean Monnet played a crucial role in directing resources and setting economic priorities. Infrastructure projects, including the expansion of the transportation network and the development of new technologies, were prioritised.

PLAQUE AFFIXED WHERE JEAN MONNET LIVED AS PLANNING COMMISSIONER DURING 1946-1952

The Trente Glorieuses (Thirty Glorious Years), from 1945 to 1975, were characterised by unprecedented economic growth, rising living standards, and the expansion of the welfare state. Social security systems, healthcare, and education were significantly improved, contributing to the overall well-being of the population.

The Algerian War

The Algerian War (1954-1962) was a pivotal conflict in the process of decolonisation and had profound consequences for France. Algeria, a French colony, had long been a focal point of tension due to the significant settler population (pieds-noirs) and the aspirations of the native Algerian population for independence.

FRENCH PATROL IN ORLEANSVILLE (CHLEF) ALGERIA IN 1957

The conflict began in 1954 with the Algerian National Liberation Front (FLN) launching a guerrilla war against French rule. The war was marked by brutal violence on both sides, including the use of torture by French forces and terrorist attacks by the FLN. The conflict deeply divided French society and exposed the limitations of the Fourth Republic.

In 1958, the political instability caused by the war led to the collapse of the Fourth Republic and the return of Charles de Gaulle to power. De Gaulle, understanding the unsustainable nature of the conflict, initiated negotiations with the FLN. The Evian Accords were signed in 1962, granting Algeria independence and ending the war.

FRANCE AND ALGERIA'S SIGNING OF THE EVIAN ACCORDS ON 18 MARCH 1962

The consequences of the Algerian War were significant. It marked the end of France's colonial empire in Africa and forced the country to confront the realities of decolonisation. The war also left deep scars on French society, including the reintegration of pieds-noirs and Harkis (Algerians who had fought for France), and a legacy of trauma and division.

Charles de Gaulle

The return of Charles de Gaulle to power in 1958 led to the establishment of the Fifth Republic, characterised by a strong executive branch designed to ensure stability and prevent the political paralysis that had plagued the Fourth Republic. De Gaulle became the first President of the Fifth Republic, a position he held until 1969.

CHARLES DE GAULLE BACK TO POWER IN 1958

De Gaulle's policies, known as Gaullism, were marked by a strong emphasis on national sovereignty, economic modernisation, and an independent foreign policy. Domestically, de Gaulle pursued significant reforms, including the decentralisation of administrative powers and the promotion of technological advancements. The French nuclear programme was developed during his tenure, establishing France as a nuclear power.

In foreign policy, de Gaulle sought to assert France's independence from the superpowers, particularly the United States and the Soviet Union. He withdrew France from NATO's integrated military command in 1966, emphasising an independent defence policy. De Gaulle also promoted European integration, though he advocated for a Europe of sovereign states rather than a supranational entity.

De Gaulle's presidency faced significant challenges, including the May 1968 protests, a series of massive demonstrations and strikes that highlighted widespread dissatisfaction with the political and social status quo. Although de Gaulle managed to restore order and win the subsequent elections, the protests marked a turning point, leading to his resignation in 1969.

Social Changes

The May 1968 protests were a watershed moment in French history, marking a period of profound social upheaval and transformation. What began as a student protest against poor university conditions and the authoritarian nature of the educational system quickly escalated into a nationwide movement that involved workers, intellectuals, artists, and various social groups, reflecting deep-seated discontent across French society.

In Bordeaux and other major cities, the protests were driven by a combination of factors. Chief among these were dissatisfaction with the authoritarian educational system, opposition to rampant consumerism and capitalist values, and a widespread desire for greater personal freedoms and social justice. Iconic slogans such as "Sous les pavés, la plage!" ("Under the cobblestones, the beach!") encapsulated the spirit of rebellion, embodying the quest for a new and more egalitarian social order.

MAY 1968 DEMONSTRATIONS IN BORDEAUX

The movement rapidly gained momentum, leading to widespread strikes that involved millions of workers and brought the French economy to a standstill. Factories, transportation networks, and even government offices were paralyzed, illustrating the depth of the crisis. Although President Charles de Gaulle's government eventually restored order, the impact of the protests was far-reaching and enduring.

The May 1968 protests prompted significant social reforms. These included substantial changes in the education system aimed at increasing accessibility and reducing authoritarian practices, improvements in workers' rights that bolstered protections and benefits, and the promotion of gender equality which advanced the feminist movement.

The transformation of French society in the post-war period was marked by rapid urbanisation, the proliferation of a consumer culture, and evolving social norms. The role of women in society saw significant changes, with increased participation in the workforce and a growing feminist movement that advocated for equal rights and opportunities. Immigration also played a crucial role in shaping the social landscape, as France evolved into a more multicultural society.

In the decades that followed, France continued to navigate the challenges and opportunities presented by modernisation, globalisation, and ongoing social change. The Fifth Republic, with its robust institutional framework and capacity for reform, proved adaptable to these evolving dynamics.

SUMMARY:

From the aftermath of World War II to the present, France's journey has been one of reconstruction, decolonisation, political transformation, and profound social change. The legacies of these historical processes continue to shape the nation's identity and its place in the world.

PEOPLE:

Charles de Gaulle (1890-1970) - Leader of the Free French Forces during World War II, founder of the Fifth Republic, and its first President. He played a crucial role in shaping modern France.

Simone Veil (1927-2017) - Holocaust survivor and influential politician, known for her role in legalising abortion in France as Minister of Health in 1975.

Jean Monnet (1888-1979) - Economist and diplomat, a key architect of European integration and the European Union.

PLACES:

Paris - Continues to be the political, economic, and cultural heart of France, central to post-war reconstruction, protests, and policy changes.

Versailles - Symbolic location for major political events, including the formation of the Fifth Republic.

Algiers - Capital of French Algeria, crucial during the Algerian War of Independence, leading to significant political changes in France.

Élysée Palace - Official residence of the French President, the centre of executive power.

Strasbourg - Home to several key European institutions, reflecting France's commitment to European integration.

EVENTS:

Liberation of France (1944) - The country was liberated from Nazi occupation, marking the end of World War II in France.

Founding of the Fourth Republic (1946) - Established after World War II, it faced political instability and economic challenges, leading to its eventual collapse.

Algerian War of Independence (1954-1962) - A brutal conflict leading to Algeria's independence and significant political changes in France, including the collapse of the Fourth Republic.
Establishment of the Fifth Republic (1958) - Charles de Gaulle founded the Fifth Republic with a new constitution, strengthening the executive branch and providing political stability.
May 1968 Protests - A period of civil unrest marked by widespread protests and strikes, leading to social and cultural changes.
European Integration - France was a founding member of the European Coal and Steel Community (1951), the European Economic Community (1957), and later the European Union, playing a key role in European integration.
Economic Modernisation - Post-war reconstruction and economic reforms transformed France into a modern industrial economy, including the "Trente Glorieuses" (Thirty Glorious Years) of economic growth.
End of Colonial Empire - Decolonisation in Africa and Asia, with significant events like the independence of Algeria (1962) and subsequent political and social impacts.
Oil Crises (1973, 1979) - Economic shocks that challenged the French economy, leading to policy changes and the end of the post-war economic boom.
Social Reforms - Various reforms including the legalisation of abortion (1975) and the abolition of the death penalty (1981).

CHAPTER 11

CONTEMPORARY FRANCE

1981 - Present

France has been a driving force in the process of European integration, playing a pivotal role in the establishment and evolution of the European Union (EU). The 1980s marked a significant period of consolidation and expansion for the European project, with France actively shaping its direction.

European Integration

France has been a driving force in the process of European integration, playing a pivotal role in the establishment and evolution of the European Union (EU). The 1980s marked a significant period of consolidation and expansion for the European project, with France actively shaping its direction.

In 1981, François Mitterrand became President of France, serving two terms until 1995. His presidency saw the strengthening of Franco-German relations, particularly with German Chancellor Helmut Kohl. This partnership was crucial in advancing European integration. The Single European Act of 1986, which aimed to create a single market by 1992, was a significant milestone during this period.

PRESIDENT FRANÇOIS MITTERRAND IN 1983

The 1992 Maastricht Treaty, formally known as the Treaty on European Union, was a landmark agreement that established the EU and paved the way for the creation of the euro. France was instrumental in drafting and promoting the treaty, which sought to deepen economic and political integration among member states. The French public narrowly approved the treaty in a referendum, reflecting the mixed feelings about deeper integration.

THE SIGNING OF THE MAASTRICHT TREATY IN 1992

France adopted the euro in 1999, becoming one of the founding members of the Eurozone. The euro's introduction was a major step towards economic unity, although it also brought challenges related to fiscal policy coordination and economic disparities among member states.

Throughout the 2000s and 2010s, France has consistently advocated for a stronger, more cohesive European Union. French leaders, including Presidents Jacques Chirac, Nicolas Sarkozy, François Hollande, and Emmanuel Macron, have all emphasised the importance of a united Europe in addressing global challenges. Each of these leaders has championed the idea that a united Europe is better equipped to tackle issues such as climate change, economic instability, and geopolitical tensions. Emmanuel Macron, in particular, has been a vocal proponent of EU reform and deeper integration, calling for increased cooperation on critical issues such as defence, migration, and economic policy. Macron has frequently highlighted the necessity of solidarity and shared sovereignty among EU member states to ensure the region's stability and prosperity in a rapidly changing world.

Modern Challenges

Contemporary France faces a range of modern challenges, including economic issues, immigration, and questions of national identity.

Economic issues have been a persistent concern. The 2008 global financial crisis and subsequent eurozone crisis significantly impacted the French economy, leading to slow growth, high unemployment, and increasing public debt. Successive governments have implemented various reforms aimed at boosting competitiveness, reducing unemployment, and controlling public spending. Labour market reforms, pension system changes, and tax policies have been contentious but necessary steps to revitalise the economy.

IMMIGRATION POLARISED IN MODERN TIMES

Immigration has also been a significant and polarising issue. France, with its colonial history and geographic position, has long been a destination for immigrants from Africa, the Middle East, and Eastern Europe. The influx of immigrants has enriched French culture and economy but has also raised challenges related to integration, social cohesion, and national identity. The rise of populist and far-right movements, exemplified by the National Front (now National Rally) led by Marine Le Pen, has brought immigration and identity politics to the forefront of national discourse.

MARINE LE PEN LEADER OF THE NATIONAL RALLY

National identity remains a complex and evolving concept in contemporary France. The country's commitment to secularism (laïcité) has been tested by debates over religious symbols, particularly Islamic headscarves, in public spaces and institutions. Terrorist attacks in the 2010s, including the Charlie Hebdo attack in 2015 and the Bataclan theatre attack the same year, have intensified discussions about security, immigration, and the integration of Muslim communities. These events have prompted government actions to bolster counter-terrorism efforts and address radicalisation while also raising concerns about civil liberties and discrimination.

THE SCENE AT THE SHOOTING AT CHARLIE HEBDO'S OFFICE IN 2015

Current Events

Recent political developments in France reflect a dynamic and often tumultuous landscape. The 2017 presidential election marked a significant shift, with the election of Emmanuel Macron, a centrist candidate who founded the party La République En Marche!. Macron's victory was notable for its rejection of traditional party structures and its promise of sweeping reforms.

Macron's presidency has been marked by ambitious domestic and international agendas. Domestically, he has pursued labour market reforms, tax cuts, and measures to reduce public spending, often facing strong opposition from unions and protest movements such as the Gilets Jaunes (Yellow Vests). This grassroots movement, which began in 2018, protested against fuel taxes and economic inequality, highlighting widespread discontent with Macron's policies and perceived elitism.

YELLOW VEST PROTESTS AGAINST MACRON'S POLICIES 2018

Internationally, Macron has positioned France as a key player in global affairs, advocating for a stronger and more united EU, addressing climate change, and promoting multilateralism. His foreign policy initiatives have included efforts to mediate conflicts, strengthen EU defence capabilities, and enhance France's role in international organisations.

Culturally, contemporary France continues to be a vibrant and influential force. The country remains a global centre for art, fashion, literature, and cinema. Paris Fashion Week, the Cannes Film Festival, and numerous art exhibitions showcase France's ongoing contributions to global culture. French cuisine, recognised by UNESCO as an intangible cultural heritage, continues to evolve while maintaining its traditional roots.

Recent years have also seen the rise of new cultural trends and movements. The influence of digital technology and social media has transformed the cultural landscape, impacting everything from media consumption to political activism. The MeToo movement found resonance in France, sparking important discussions about gender equality and sexual harassment. Additionally, issues of environmental sustainability and climate action have gained prominence, with increasing public awareness and activism driving policy changes.

EMMANUEL MACRON FRANCE'S PRESIDENT SINCE 2017

French Political Developments in 2024

In 2024, France's political landscape is marked by significant uncertainty. Recent developments show the leftist New Popular Front coalition leading in parliamentary seats, preventing the far-right from gaining power outright. However, they did not secure a majority, leaving France in an unprecedented situation. Prime Minister Gabriel Attal warned that the National Rally is "at the gates of power." Meanwhile, thousands protested in Paris against the far-right's strong performance.

As France heads to the second round of the election, the nation faces a critical juncture. The results will determine the National Assembly's composition and could lead to a "cohabitation" scenario if the National Rally secures a parliamentary majority. The future direction of France hangs in the balance, shaped by the outcomes of this pivotal election year.

SUMMARY:

France has been a central force in European integration, significantly contributing to the establishment and evolution of the European Union, particularly during the 1980s and 1990s with key milestones like the Single European Act and the Maastricht Treaty. Despite facing modern challenges such as economic issues, immigration, and national identity debates, France has remained a proponent of a stronger EU under various leaders, including Emmanuel Macron. Currently, the political landscape in 2024 is marked by uncertainty due to early parliamentary elections, with the leftist New Popular Front coalition leading but lacking a majority, leaving the potential for a far-right National Rally rise and a complex political future.

PEOPLE:

François Mitterrand (1916-1996) - President of France from 1981 to 1995, known for his socialist policies, European integration efforts, and the abolition of the death penalty.

Jacques Chirac (1932-2019) - President from 1995 to 2007, focused on economic reforms, cultural policy, and opposing the Iraq War.

Nicolas Sarkozy (1955-) - President from 2007 to 2012, known for his economic reforms, immigration policies, and international diplomacy.

François Hollande (1954-) - President from 2012 to 2017, faced economic challenges, implemented social reforms, and responded to terrorism threats.

Emmanuel Macron (1977-) - Current President since 2017, founder of La République En Marche!, advocating economic reform, EU integration, and social issues.

Angela Merkel - Chancellor of Germany, played a significant role in Franco-German relations and European Union policies during this period.

Marine Le Pen (1968-) - Leader of the National Rally (formerly National Front), a prominent figure in French politics advocating nationalist and anti-EU positions.

Christine Lagarde (1956-) - Former French Minister of Finance, now President of the European Central Bank, influential in global financial policies.

PLACES:

Paris - The political, economic, and cultural capital of France, central to national and international events, protests, and policies.

European Union Institutions - France plays a significant role in EU governance, with institutions in Brussels and Strasbourg shaping European policies.

Toulouse - A centre of aerospace industry and research, reflecting France's technological achievements and economic diversity.

Marseille - A major port city, cultural hub, and centre of immigration, highlighting France's Mediterranean connection and multicultural society.

EVENTS:

Maastricht Treaty (1992) - Established the European Union, shaping France's role in European integration and governance.

1995 Paris Metro bombings - Terrorist attacks targeting the Paris Metro system, leading to increased security measures and counter-terrorism efforts.

2003 European Constitution Referendum - France held a referendum on the proposed European Constitution, which was rejected, influencing EU institutional reforms.

Financial Crisis (2008) - Global economic downturn affecting France, prompting economic reforms and challenges in financial stability.

Charlie Hebdo Shooting (2015) - Terrorist attack on the offices of the satirical magazine Charlie Hebdo, sparking national and international debates on free speech and security.

Paris Agreement (2015) - International climate accord aiming to combat climate change, signed in Paris and significant for French environmental policy.

Yellow Vests Movement (2018) - Protests against economic inequality and government policies, highlighting social discontent and policy responses.

COVID-19 Pandemic (2020-) - France, like the rest of the world, faced significant challenges in public health, economic stability, and social cohesion during the pandemic.

CHAPTER 12

COLONIAL LEGACY TO CONTEMPORARY LEADERSHIP

Colonial Era - Present

The concept of Francophonie encompasses the global community of French-speaking people and the cultural, linguistic, and political influence of France around the world. This influence stems from France's extensive colonial empire, its cultural diplomacy, and its commitment to promoting the French language and culture internationally.

Francophonie

During the colonial era, France established vast territories across Africa, Asia, the Americas, and the Pacific. Major colonies included Algeria, Morocco, Tunisia, Senegal, Vietnam (then part of French Indochina), and the Caribbean islands of Martinique and Guadeloupe. These colonies not only expanded France's political and economic reach but also disseminated French language and culture. Education systems in these colonies often centred around French curricula, and French became a lingua franca in many regions.

Post-decolonisation, the legacy of French influence persisted. The establishment of the Organisation Internationale de la Francophonie (OIF) in 1970 institutionalised the global community of French-speaking nations. The OIF promotes French language and culture, educational cooperation, and political dialogue among its 88 member states and governments. It serves as a platform for fostering solidarity and mutual development among Francophone countries.

The French language remains a global language of diplomacy, education, and culture. French is one of the official languages of the United Nations, the European Union, NATO, and other international organisations. It is spoken by millions worldwide, with significant Francophone populations in Africa, North America, the Caribbean, and parts of Asia. The annual International Francophonie Day, celebrated on 20 March, highlights the cultural diversity and linguistic heritage of the Francophone world.

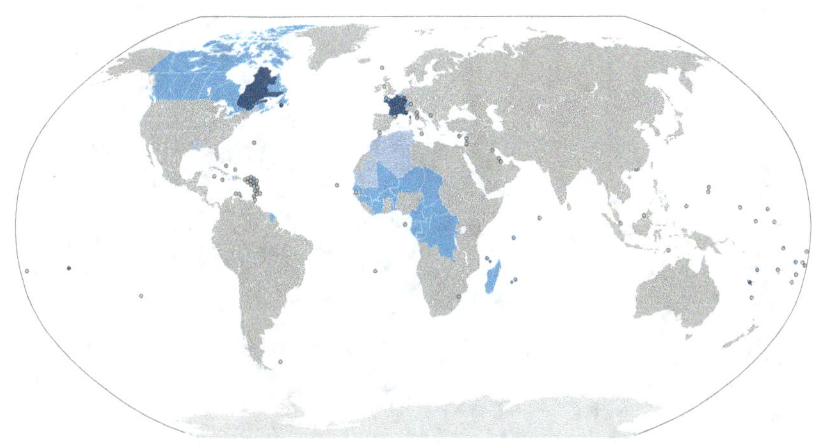

MAP OF THE FRANCOPHONE WORLD

Culturally, France's influence is evident in literature, cinema, art, and cuisine. French literature has produced global literary giants such as Victor Hugo, Marcel Proust, and Albert Camus. French cinema, with its rich tradition of auteurs like François Truffaut and Jean-Luc Godard, continues to inspire filmmakers worldwide. The culinary arts, epitomised by French cuisine, have set global standards for fine dining and culinary excellence.

International Relations

France has played a significant role in global politics, marked by its active participation in international organisations and its commitment to multilateralism. As a permanent member of the United Nations Security Council and a founding member of NATO and the European Union, France wields considerable influence on the global stage.

United Nations

GENERAL ASSEMBLY OF THE UNITED NATIONS

France has been a staunch supporter of the United Nations since its inception in 1945. As one of the five permanent members of the UN Security Council, France has the power to veto resolutions and plays a critical role in maintaining international peace and security. France has been involved in various peacekeeping missions and has advocated for international cooperation on issues such as human rights, climate change, and sustainable development.

NATO

France was a founding member of the North Atlantic Treaty Organisation (NATO) in 1949. Although it withdrew from NATO's integrated military command in 1966 under President Charles de Gaulle to assert greater independence in defence policy, France remained a member of the alliance. In 2009, under President Nicolas Sarkozy, France fully rejoined NATO's military command structure, reaffirming its commitment to collective security and transatlantic cooperation. France has contributed to various NATO operations, including those in Afghanistan, Kosovo, and Libya.

NATO EMBLEM

European Union

France has been a driving force behind European integration, advocating for a strong and united Europe. It played a pivotal role in the creation of the European Economic Community (EEC) in 1957, which later evolved into the European Union (EU). French leaders have consistently supported policies aimed at deepening economic, political, and security cooperation within the EU. France's commitment to the euro and the Schengen Area reflects its belief in the benefits of European unity.

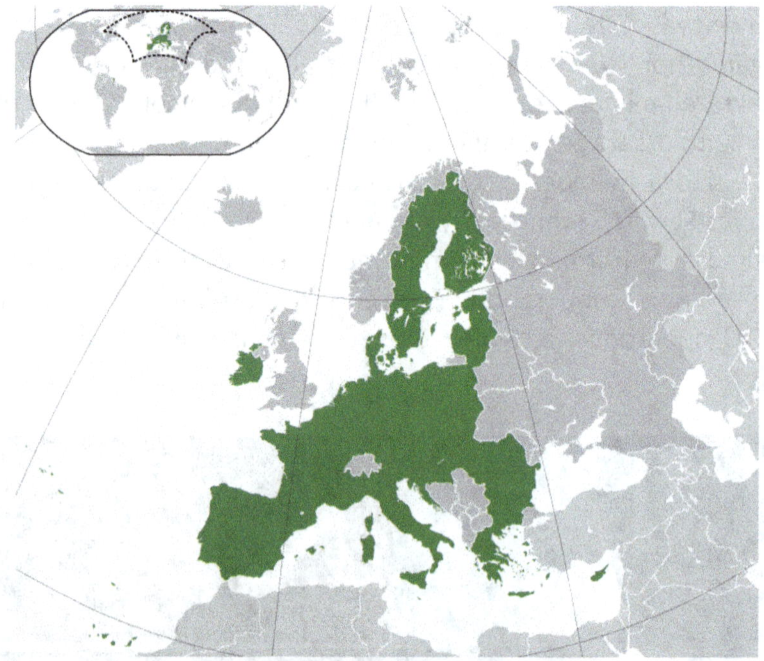

MAP OF EUROPEAN UNION MEMBERS

Francafrique

France has maintained close ties with its former African colonies, a policy often referred to as Francafrique. This relationship involves economic, political, and military cooperation, though it has also been criticised for perpetuating neo-colonial dynamics. France has intervened militarily in African conflicts, such as in Mali and the Central African Republic, to stabilise regions and combat terrorism. French development aid and economic investments in Africa continue to be significant.

Global Challenges

France has taken a proactive stance on global issues such as climate change, terrorism, and international trade. The Paris Agreement, adopted in 2015, is a landmark international treaty on climate change that underscores France's leadership in environmental diplomacy. France has also been at the forefront of counter-terrorism efforts, both domestically and internationally, particularly following a series of terrorist attacks in the 2010s.

THE PARIS AGREEMENT, ADOPTED IN 2015

In the realm of international trade, France advocates for a rules-based multilateral trading system and actively participates in the World Trade Organisation (WTO). French leaders have also promoted cultural diplomacy through initiatives such as the Institut Français and the global network of Alliances Françaises, which promote French language and culture worldwide.

Recent Political Developments: France's recent political landscape has been marked by the presidency of Emmanuel Macron, who has sought to revitalise France's role in Europe and the world. Macron's administration has focused on economic reforms, strengthening the EU, and addressing global challenges such as climate change and international security. His leadership has also faced significant domestic challenges, including the Yellow Vests movement and debates over immigration and social policy.

SUMMARY:

France's global influence is rooted in its historical legacy as a colonial power, its commitment to promoting the French language and culture, and its active participation in international organisations. Through its diplomatic, economic, and cultural initiatives, France continues to shape global affairs and maintain its status as a key player on the world stage.

PEOPLE:

Colonial Era:

Louis XIV (1638-1715) - Expanded French colonial holdings in North America, Africa, and Asia during his reign, laying foundations for French colonialism.

Joseph Gallieni (1849-1916) - Military leader and colonial administrator, known for his role in expanding French territories in Africa, especially in Madagascar.

Jules Ferry (1832-1893) - Prime Minister and advocate of colonial expansion, his policies led to significant French territorial gains in Africa and Southeast Asia.

20th Century:

Charles de Gaulle (1890-1970) - Leader of the Free French Forces during World War II, founder of the Fifth Republic, and advocate for decolonisation.

François Mitterrand (1916-1996) - President from 1981 to 1995, oversaw the independence of several African colonies and managed the transition from colonialism to cooperation.

Jacques Chirac (1932-2019) - President from 1995 to 2007, sought to strengthen ties with former colonies while acknowledging the colonial past.

21st Century:

Nicolas Sarkozy (1955-) - President from 2007 to 2012, advocated for a partnership of equals with former colonies, addressing historical grievances.

François Hollande (1954-) - President from 2012 to 2017, focused on economic cooperation and development aid in former French colonies.

Emmanuel Macron (1977-) - Current President since 2017, committed to fostering partnerships with Africa based on mutual respect and cooperation.

Colonial Era:

Algiers, Algeria - Capital of French Algeria, central to French colonial administration and resistance movements.

Dakar, Senegal - A major port and administrative centre during French colonial rule in West Africa.

Hanoi, Vietnam - Capital of French Indochina, symbolising French colonial influence in Southeast Asia.

20th Century:

Paris, France - Administrative centre and policy hub for French colonial administration and later, post-colonial relations.

Yamoussoukro, Côte d'Ivoire - Symbolic city in Africa, highlighting Franco-Ivorian relations and economic ties.

21st Century:

Brussels, Belgium - European Union headquarters, influencing French and EU policy towards former colonies.

Ouagadougou, Burkina Faso - Capital city representing French-West African relations and regional cooperation.

EVENTS:

Colonial Era:

Scramble for Africa (late 19th century) - Intense competition among European powers, including France, for control of African territories.

First Indochina War (1946-1954) - Conflict between French forces and Vietnamese nationalists, leading to French withdrawal from Vietnam.

20th Century:

Algerian War of Independence (1954-1962) - Violent conflict resulting in Algeria's independence from French rule, impacting French politics and society.

Decolonisation in Africa (1960s) - Wave of independence movements leading to the end of French colonial rule in many African countries.

21st Century:

Franco-African Summits - Regular meetings between French and African leaders to discuss economic cooperation, security, and development.

Migration and Integration - Issues surrounding migration from former colonies to France, shaping social policies and political discourse.

Globalisation and Economic Partnerships - Efforts to foster economic ties and cooperation between France and its former colonies in a globalised world.

Cultural Exchange and Influence - Continued French cultural influence in former colonies, including language, education, and arts.

Security Cooperation - Collaboration on regional security issues, counter-terrorism efforts, and peacekeeping operations.

Human Rights and Governance - Promotion of democratic governance, human rights, and rule of law in former French territories.

FRANKISH KINGDOM (486–843)

MEROVINGIAN DYNASTY

Clovis I (481–511) - First King of the Franks to unite all the Frankish tribes under one ruler.

Chlothar I (511–561) - Expanded the Frankish kingdom after Clovis I.

Chlothar II (584–629) - Expanded the kingdom and reduced the power of the nobility.

Dagobert I (629–639) - One of the last effective Merovingian kings.

Childeric III (743–751) - Last Merovingian king, deposed by Pepin the Short.

CAROLINGIAN DYNASTY

Pepin the Short (751–768) - First Carolingian king of the Franks.

Charlemagne (Charles the Great) (768–814) - Emperor who expanded the Frankish state into a large empire.

Louis the Pious (814–840) - Charlemagne's son, struggled to maintain the empire's unity.

Charles the Bald (843–877) - Ruled West Francia after the Treaty of Verdun.

WEST FRANCIA (843–987)

Charles the Bald (843–877) - Continued to rule after the division of the Carolingian Empire.

Louis the Stammerer (877–879) - Son of Charles the Bald, short reign.

Louis III and Carloman II (879–882) - Co-rulers after their father's death.

Charles the Fat (884–888) - Briefly reunited the Carolingian Empire.

Odo of Paris (888–898) - Non-Carolingian king elected by the nobility.
Charles the Simple (898–922) - Lost significant territory to Viking invasions.
Robert I (922–923) - Elected king, killed in battle.
Rudolph of France (923–936) - Duke of Burgundy, elected as king.
Louis IV (936–954) - Son of Charles the Simple, known as Louis d'Outremer.
Lothair (954–986) - Continued struggles with the nobility.
Louis V (986–987) - Last Carolingian king, died without an heir.

CAPETIAN DYNASTY (987–1328)

Hugh Capet (987–996) - Founder of the Capetian dynasty.
Robert II (Robert the Pious) (996–1031) - Known for his piety.
Henry I (1031–1060) - Struggled with internal revolts.
Philip I (1060–1108) - Increased royal territories.
Louis VI (Louis the Fat) (1108–1137) - Strengthened royal authority.
Louis VII (Louis the Young) (1137–1180) - Participated in the Second Crusade.
Philip II Augustus (1180–1223) - Expanded French territories significantly.
Louis VIII (Louis the Lion) (1223–1226) - Short reign, crusader.
Louis IX (Saint Louis) (1226–1270) - Canonised as a saint, known for his justice and crusades.
Philip III (Philip the Bold) (1270–1285) - Expanded French territories through marriage and inheritance.
Philip IV (Philip the Fair) (1285–1314) - Strengthened the monarchy, expelled the Jews, and suppressed the Templars.
Louis X (the Quarreler) (1314–1316) - Short reign, issues with succession.
John I (the Posthumous) (1316) - Reigned for five days.
Philip V (the Tall) (1316–1322) - Younger son of Philip IV, continued father's policies.

Charles IV (the Fair) (1322–1328) - Last direct Capetian king, his death led to the Hundred Years' War.

**VALOIS DYNASTY** (1328–1589)
Philip VI (1328–1350) - First Valois king, began the Hundred Years' War.
John II (John the Good) (1350–1364) - Captured during the Battle of Poitiers.
Charles V (Charles the Wise) (1364–1380) - Rebuilt France after initial losses in the Hundred Years' War.
Charles VI (Charles the Mad) (1380–1422) - Period of mental illness and civil war.
Charles VII (the Victorious) (1422–1461) - Regained territories from the English with Joan of Arc's help.
Louis XI (the Prudent) (1461–1483) - Strengthened royal authority and reduced the power of the nobles.
Charles VIII (the Affable) (1483–1498) - Initiated the Italian Wars.
Louis XII (Father of the People) (1498–1515) - Continued the Italian Wars, popular king.
Francis I (1515–1547) - Renaissance king, patron of the arts, continued Italian Wars.
Henry II (1547–1559) - Strengthened central authority, continued conflicts with the Habsburgs.
Francis II (1559–1560) - Short reign, married to Mary, Queen of Scots.
Charles IX (1560–1574) - His reign saw the Massacre of St. Bartholomew's Day.
Henry III (1574–1589) - Last Valois king, assassinated during the Wars of Religion.

**BOURBON DYNASTY** (1589–1792, 1814–1830)
Henry IV (1589–1610) - First Bourbon king, issued the Edict of Nantes.

Louis XIII (the Just) (1610–1643) - Worked with Cardinal Richelieu to strengthen the monarchy.
Louis XIV (the Sun King) (1643–1715) - Known for his absolute monarchy and the construction of Versailles.
Louis XV (the Beloved) (1715–1774) - Long but ineffective reign, leading to financial crisis.
Louis XVI (1774–1792) - Last king before the French Revolution, executed in 1793.

FIRST REPUBLIC (1792–1804)

National Convention (1792–1795) - Led by various figures including Maximilien Robespierre during the Reign of Terror.
Directory (1795–1799) - Five-member committee that governed before Napoleon's rise.
Napoleon Bonaparte (1799–1804) - Rose to power as First Consul before becoming Emperor.

FIRST EMPIRE (1804–1814/1815)

Napoleon I (Napoleon Bonaparte) (1804–1814, 1815) - Declared himself Emperor of the French, abdicated after defeat, returned for the Hundred Days before final defeat at Waterloo.

BOURBON RESTORATION (1814–1830)

Louis XVIII (1814–1824) - Restored to the throne after Napoleon's abdication.
Charles X (1824–1830) - Last Bourbon king, abdicated after the July Revolution.

JULY MONARCHY (1830–1848)

Louis-Philippe I (1830–1848) - "Citizen King," overthrown during the February Revolution.

SECOND REPUBLIC (1848–1852)

Louis-Napoleon Bonaparte (1848–1852) - Elected President, later became Napoleon III.

SECOND EMPIRE (1852–1870)

Napoleon III (Louis-Napoleon) (1852–1870) - Declared himself Emperor, defeated in the Franco-Prussian War.

THIRD REPUBLIC (1870–1940)

Adolphe Thiers (1871–1873) - First President of the Third Republic.
Patrice de MacMahon (1873–1879) - Second President, resigned after political crisis.
Jules Grévy (1879–1887) - Served two terms, resigned due to scandal.
Sadi Carnot (1887–1894) - Assassinated while in office.
Jean Casimir-Perier (1894–1895) - Resigned after a few months.
Félix Faure (1895–1899) - Died in office.
Émile Loubet (1899–1906) - Oversaw the Dreyfus Affair resolution.
Armand Fallières (1906–1913) - Promoted social reforms.
Raymond Poincaré (1913–1920) - President during World War I.
Paul Deschanel (1920) - Short term due to health issues.
Alexandre Millerand (1920–1924) - Resigned after a political dispute.
Gaston Doumergue (1924–1931) - Promoted conservative policies.
Paul Doumer (1931–1932) - Assassinated while in office.
Albert Lebrun (1932–1940) - Last President before World War II and the fall of France.

VICHY FRANCE (1940–1944)

Philippe Pétain (1940–1944) - Head of State of the Vichy government collaborating with Nazi Germany.

**PROVISIONAL GOVERNMENT (1944–1946)**

Charles de Gaulle (1944–1946) - Leader of the Free French Forces, headed the Provisional Government after liberation.

**FOURTH REPUBLIC (1946–1958)**

Vincent Auriol (1947–1954) - First President of the Fourth Republic.

René Coty (1954–1959) - Last President of the Fourth Republic.

**FIFTH REPUBLIC (1958–PRESENT)**

Charles de Gaulle (1959–1969) - First President of the Fifth Republic, established a strong executive.

Georges Pompidou (1969–1974) - Continued Gaullist policies, focused on economic modernisation.

Valéry Giscard d'Estaing (1974–1981) - Promoted liberal economic policies.

François Mitterrand (1981–1995) - Longest-serving President of the Fifth Republic, implemented socialist policies.

Jacques Chirac (1995–2007) - Known for his opposition to the Iraq War, promoted European integration.

Nicolas Sarkozy (2007–2012) - Focused on economic reform and improving France's international standing.

François Hollande (2012–2017) - Faced economic challenges and terrorist attacks.

Emmanuel Macron (2017–Present) - Current President, first elected in 2017, focusing on economic reform and international diplomacy.

MEDIEVAL PERIOD (5TH TO 15TH CENTURY)

Charlemagne and the Carolingian Renaissance (c. 800) - Charlemagne's reign saw a revival of art, culture, and learning based on classical models.
This period laid the foundation for many educational and cultural traditions in France.

Gothic Architecture (12th-16th century) - Development of Gothic architecture, epitomised by cathedrals like Notre-Dame de Paris (1163), Chartres Cathedral (1194), and Amiens Cathedral (1220).
Gothic architecture introduced innovations such as the pointed arch, ribbed vault, and flying buttress.

RENAISSANCE (15TH TO 17TH CENTURY)

François I and the French Renaissance (1515-1547) - Patronage of the arts and humanism; development of châteaux like Chambord and Fontainebleau.
François I encouraged the spread of Renaissance art and ideas in France.

Birth of French Cuisine (16th century) - Development of haute cuisine with an emphasis on sauces, fresh ingredients, and presentation.
French cuisine began to take shape under chefs such as François Pierre La Varenne.

17TH CENTURY

Louis XIV and the Age of Absolutism (1643-1715) - Establishment of the Palace of Versailles as the centre of political power and culture.
Versailles became a symbol of French royal grandeur and artistic achievement.

18th Century

Enlightenment (18th century) - Intellectual and philosophical movement promoting reason, science, and individual rights. Thinkers like Voltaire, Rousseau, and Diderot contributed to the French Enlightenment.

Establishment of the Académie Française (1635) - Founded by Cardinal Richelieu to regulate the French language and preserve its purity. The Académie Française remains an important institution in French cultural heritage.

19th Century

Napoleon and the Napoleonic Code (1804) - Introduction of the Napoleonic Code, which influenced legal systems worldwide. The Code civil established principles of civil law that are still in use in France today.

Impressionism (Late 19th century) - Artistic movement characterised by a focus on light and everyday scenes, with artists like Claude Monet and Edgar Degas. Impressionism revolutionised painting and contributed to modern art.

20th Century

French Cinema (Early 20th century onwards) - Pioneering contributions to cinema, including the work of directors like Georges Méliès and the Lumière brothers. France continues to be a major centre for film, with the Cannes Film Festival being one of the most prestigious in the world.

Moulin Rouge and the Belle Époque (1889) - Establishment of the Moulin Rouge, symbolising the vibrant cultural life of the Belle Époque. The period was marked by artistic and social flourishing, with cabarets, theatres, and cafes thriving in Paris.

Tour de France (1903) - Inauguration of the world's most famous cycling race.The Tour de France has become an integral part of French sporting tradition and culture.

French Cuisine and UNESCO (2010) - French gastronomy was inscribed on the UNESCO Intangible Cultural Heritage list. Recognised for its social and cultural significance, French cuisine continues to influence global culinary practices.

21ST CENTURY

Fête de la Musique (1982) - Annual music festival held on the summer solstice, celebrating music in all its forms. Founded by the French Ministry of Culture, it has become a global celebration observed in many countries.

Paris Fashion Week - One of the "Big Four" fashion weeks, showcasing the latest in haute couture and ready-to-wear collections. Paris Fashion Week remains a leading event in the global fashion calendar, influencing trends worldwide.

Bastille Day (July 14) - National holiday commemorating the French Revolution and the storming of the Bastille in 1789. Celebrated with parades, fireworks, and parties, it symbolises French national pride and unity.

1600s

Molière (1622-1673) - Playwright, actor, and poet; known for his comedies such as "Tartuffe," "The Misanthrope," and "The Imaginary Invalid." Molière is considered one of the greatest masters of comedy in Western literature.

1700s

Voltaire (1694-1778) - Writer, historian, and philosopher; known for works such as "Candide" and "Letters on the English." Voltaire was a leading figure of the Enlightenment, advocating for civil liberties and freedom of expression.

1800s

Victor Hugo (1802-1885) - Poet, novelist, and dramatist; best known for "Les Misérables" and "The Hunchback of Notre-Dame." Hugo's works had a profound impact on French literature and he was also a political activist.

Édouard Manet (1832-1883) - Painter; one of the first 19th-century artists to paint modern life, known for "Olympia" and "Le Déjeuner sur l'herbe." Manet's work was crucial in the transition from Realism to Impressionism.

Claude Debussy (1862-1918) - Composer; known for pioneering the Impressionist music style with works such as "Clair de Lune" and "La Mer." Debussy's innovative compositions have had a lasting influence on classical music.

1900s

Auguste and Louis Lumière (1862-1954; 1864-1948) - Filmmakers and inventors; among the first to create motion pictures with their invention, the Cinématographe. The Lumière brothers are often credited with the birth of cinema.

Sidonie-Gabrielle Colette (1873-1954) - Novelist; known for works such as "Gigi" and "Claudine" series. Colette was a pioneering female writer who explored themes of female independence and sexuality.

Jean Cocteau (1889-1963) - Poet, novelist, playwright, artist, and filmmaker; known for films such as "La Belle et la Bête" and "Orphée." Cocteau was a prominent figure in avant-garde art and a versatile contributor to multiple art forms.

Edith Piaf (1915-1963) - Singer and cultural icon; known for songs like "La Vie en rose" and "Non, je ne regrette rien." Piaf's powerful voice and emotive performances made her one of France's greatest musical legends.

1950s

Brigitte Bardot (1934-) - Actress, singer, and model; became an international sex symbol with films like "And God Created Woman." Bardot is also known for her later work as an animal rights activist.

1960s

François Truffaut (1932-1984) - Filmmaker; a key figure in the French New Wave, known for films like "The 400 Blows" and "Jules and Jim." Truffaut's innovative storytelling and cinematic techniques greatly influenced modern filmmaking.

1970s

Serge Gainsbourg (1928-1991) - Singer, songwriter, and actor; known for provocative songs like "Je t'aime... moi non plus." Gainsbourg was a controversial and influential figure in French music and culture.

Catherine Deneuve (1943-) - Actress; known for roles in films such as "The Umbrellas of Cherbourg" and "Belle de Jour." Deneuve is regarded as one of the greatest European actresses.

1980s

Jean-Paul Gaultier (1952-) - Fashion designer; known for his avant-garde and innovative designs. Gaultier's work has had a significant impact on fashion, known for popularising the "man-skirt" and Madonna's iconic cone bra.

2000s

Jean-Pierre Jeunet (1953-) - Filmmaker; known for directing "Amélie" and "The City of Lost Children." Jeunet's distinctive visual style and storytelling have earned him international acclaim.

Marion Cotillard (1975-) - Actress; won an Academy Award for her role in "La Vie en Rose," and has starred in numerous critically acclaimed films. Cotillard is celebrated for her versatility and powerful performances.

2010s

Daft Punk (1993-2021) - Electronic music duo; known for hits like "One More Time" and "Get Lucky". Daft Punk revolutionised electronic music and became global icons.

2020s

Angèle (1995-) - Singer-songwriter; known for her debut album "Brol" and hits like "Tout oublier." Angèle is one of the leading figures in contemporary French pop music.

Angèle (1995-) - Singer-songwriter; known for her debut album "Brol" and hits like "Tout oublier." Angèle is one of the leading figures in contemporary French pop music.

1900s

Jean Bouin (1888-1914) - Long-distance runner; set the world record in the 10,000 metres in 1911. Won a silver medal in the 5,000 metres at the 1912 Stockholm Olympics. Bouin's legacy is remembered through the Jean Bouin Stadium in Marseille.

1920s

Suzanne Lenglen (1899-1938) - Tennis player; won 31 championship titles, including 6 Wimbledon singles titles and 2 Olympic gold medals. Lenglen revolutionised women's tennis with her style and became an international sports icon.

1930s

Jules Ladoumègue (1906-1973) - Middle-distance runner; set world records in the 1,500 metres and mile. Ladoumègue's career was cut short by professional bans, but he remains a celebrated figure in French athletics.

1950s

Jean Borotra (1898-1994) - Tennis player; one of the "Four Musketeers" of French tennis, won multiple Grand Slam titles. Known for his distinctive style, including wearing a beret during matches.

1960s

Raymond Kopa (1931-2017) - Footballer; won the Ballon d'Or in 1958. Played for Stade de Reims and Real Madrid, winning multiple league titles and European Cups. Kopa was renowned for his dribbling and playmaking abilities.

1970s

Michel Jazy (1936-) - Middle-distance runner; set world records in the 2,000 metres and mile. Won a silver medal in the 1,500 metres at the 1960 Rome Olympics. Jazy was one of France's most successful track athletes of the 1960s.

Alain Prost (1955-) - Formula One driver; won four World Championships (1985, 1986, 1989, 1993). Known as "The Professor" for his strategic approach to racing.

1980s

Michel Platini (1955-) - Footballer; won three Ballon d'Or awards (1983, 1984, 1985). Led France to victory in the 1984 UEFA European Championship. Platini is regarded as one of the greatest footballers of all time.

Bernard Hinault (1954-) - Cyclist; won the Tour de France five times (1978, 1979, 1981, 1982, 1985). Known as "The Badger," Hinault is one of cycling's greatest champions.

1990s

Zinedine Zidane (1972-) - Footballer; led France to victory in the 1998 FIFA World Cup and UEFA Euro 2000. Won the Ballon d'Or in 1998. Zidane is celebrated for his skill, vision, and leadership on the pitch.

2000s

Marie-José Pérec (1968-) - Sprinter; won three Olympic gold medals in the 200 and 400 metres (1992, 1996). Pérec is one of the greatest female sprinters in history.

Thierry Henry (1977-) - Footballer; France's all-time leading goal scorer. Won the 1998 FIFA World Cup and UEFA Euro 2000. Henry had a prolific career with clubs like Arsenal and Barcelona.

2010s

Renaud Lavillenie (1986-) - Pole vaulter; set the world record in 2014 and won the gold medal at the 2012 London Olympics. Lavillenie is one of the most successful pole vaulters of all time.

Teddy Riner (1989-) - Judoka; won two Olympic gold medals (2012, 2016) and ten World Championships. Riner is considered one of the greatest judokas in history.

2020s

Kylian Mbappé (1998-) - Footballer; won the 2018 FIFA World Cup with France. Known for his speed and goal-scoring prowess. Mbappé is regarded as one of the best young talents in football.

INDEX

Aachen, 20, 22
Abri de Cro-Magnon, 1
Acre, 27
Afghanistan, 107
Africa, 86, 92, 97, 104, 105, 109, 111, 112, 113
Agincourt, Battle of, 39
Alcuin of York, 20
Alemanni, 16
Alesia, 5, 7, 10, 15
Alesia, Battle of, 8
Alesia, Siege of, 9
Alexander I of Russia, 58
Algeria, 68, 85, 86, 91, 92, 104, 113
Algerian War, 85, 86, 91, 92, 113
Algiers, 68, 91, 112
Americas, The, 104
Angèle, 126
Arelate (Arles), 11
Ariovistus, 9
Art Deco, 76
Arverni tribe, 7
Asia, 92, 104, 105, 111, 112
Attal, Gabriel, 101
Austerlitz, 59, 60
Avignon, 30, 31, 39
Barbarossa, Frederick, 27
Bardot, Brigitte, 124
Baron Haussmann, 66
Bastille Day, 122
Bastille, The storming of the, 53
Battle of Nations. *See* Leipzig, Battle of
Belgium, 4, 59, 112
Belle Époque, 70, 79, 121
Bibracte, 5
Bibracte, Battle of, 9
Blitzkrieg campaign, 77
Bloody Week, 66
Blum, Léon, 75
Bonaparte, Louis-Napoleon, 65
Bonaparte, Napoleon, 55, 56, 58, 61, 68, 69
Borotra, Jean, 127
Bouin, Jean, 127
Bourbon Restoration, 61, 62
Bourbons, 41, 47, 63
Bouvines, Battle of, 24, 31
Breton, André, 76
Brussels, 103
Caesar, Julius, 5, 7, 8, 9, 15
Calvin, John, 34
Camus, Albert, 105
Cannes Film Festival, 99, 121
Capetian dynasty, 23, 29, 30, 31
Caribbean, The, 104, 105
Carnac, 7
Carnac stones (Brittany), 3
Carolingian dynasty, 18
Carolingian Renaissance, 20, 120
Carolingians, 18
Catherine de' Medici, 34
Catholics, 33, 40
Celts, 3, 6
Chambord, Château de, 32, 39
Champs-Élysées, 78
Charlemagne, 18, 19, 20, 21, 22, 120

Charles IX, 35
Charles the Great. *See* Charlemgne
Charles V, 38
Charles VII, 27, 38, 39
Charles X, 62, 68, 69
Charlie Hebdo attack, 98
Chirac, Jacques, 102, 111
Christianity, 13, 17, 21, 22
Clemenceau, Georges, 80
Clermont-Ferrand, 5, 7
Climate change, 99, 103, 107, 109, 110
Clouet, François, 33
Clouet, Jean, 33
Clovis I, 16
Cocteau, Jean, 124
Colbert, Jean-Baptiste, 48
Colette, Sidonie-Gabrielle, 124
Colonia Agrippina (Cologne), 15
Commentarii de Bello Gallico, 5, 9
Concordat of Bologna, 39
Congress of Vienna, 60, 69
Cotillard, Marion, 125
COVID-19 Pandemic, 103
Crécy, Battle of, 27, 39
Crimean War, 66, 69
Crusade, The First, 26
Crusade, The Second, 27, 30, 31
Crusade, The Third, 27, 30
Curie, Marie, 80
Daft Punk, 125
d'Alembert, Jean le Rond, 52
Dalí, Salvador, 76
Danton, Georges, 58
D-Day, 78, 81, 82
de Beauharnais, Josephine, 58
De Gaulle, Charles, 78, 80, 86, 87, 88, 91, 92, 107, 111
Debussy, Claude, 123
Degas, Edgar, 70, 121
Deneuve, Catherine, 125
Diderot, Denis, 51, 121
Dordogne Valley, 2, 7
Dreyfus Affair, 81
Duke of Berry, 61
Dunkirk, 81
Edict of Nantes, 36, 40, 46, 48, 49
Edward III, 27
Eiffel Tower, 70, 71
Elba, Island of, 60
Enlightenment, The, 51, 52, 57, 121, 123
European Economic Community, 92, 108
European Union, 91, 92, 93, 101, 102, 103, 105, 106, 108, 112
Eurozone, 95
Evian Accords, The, 86
Exposition Universelle 1889, 70
Ferry, Jules, 111
Fête de la Musique (1982), 122
Fifth Republic, 87, 91, 92, 111
First Indochina War, 113
Fitzgerald, F. Scott, 76
Foch, General Ferdinand, 74

Fontainebleau, 33, 49, 120
Fontainebleau, Château de, 32, 39
Fourth Republic, 83, 86, 91, 92
Francis I, 32, 38, 39
Francis II, 35
Francis, Duke of Guise, 34
François Arouet. *See* Voltaire
Franco-Prussian War, 66, 68, 69, 70
Franks, 13, 15, 16, 21
French cinema, 106
French Cuisine, 120, 122
French Resistance, 78
French Revolution, 48, 50, 52, 58, 59, 122
French Wars of Religion, 33, 37, 38, 40, 49
Fronde, The, 43
Gallic tribes, 7, 9
Gallic Wars, 5, 7, 8, 9, 15
Gallicanism, 45
Gallieni, Joseph, 111
Gauls, 4, 9
Gaultier, Jean-Paul, 125
Gergovia, 5, 7
Germany, 4, 18, 19, 22, 34, 69, 73, 74, 78, 80, 81, 82, 102
Godard, Jean-Luc, 106
Godfrey of Bouillon, 26
Great Depression, The, 75, 81
Grotte du Vallonnet, 1
Guadeloupe, 104
Hastings, Battle of, 31
Haussmann, Georges-Eugène. *See* Baron Haussmann
Helvetii, 9
Hemingway, Ernest, 76
Henry I, 23
Henry II, 38
Henry III, 31, 35, 38
Henry IV, 35, 36, 37, 40, 41, 48, 49
Henry, Thierry, 129
Hinault, Bernard, 128
Hollande, François, 102, 111
Holy Land, The, 26, 27
Hugh Capet, 23, 30
Hugo, Victor, 68, 71, 105, 123
Huguenots, 33, 34, 36, 40, 42, 46, 48, 49
Hundred Years' War, The, 27, 29, 38, 39
Île-de-France, 23, 30
Immigration, 97
Impressionism, 121, 123
Iron Age, 4, 7
Jaurès, Jean, 80
Jazy, Michel, 128
Jean-Baptiste Poquelin. *See* Molière
Jeanneret, Charles-Édouard. *See* Le Corbusier
Jerusalem, 26, 27
Jeunet, Jean-Pierre, 125
Jews, 77
Joan of Arc, 27, 28, 38, 39
July Revolution, 62, 63, 68, 69
Kohl, Helmut, 93

Kopa, Raymond, 127
Kosovo, 107
La Rochelle, 49
La Rochelle, The Siege of, 42, 49
Ladoumègue, Jules, 127
Lagarde, Christine, 102
Lascaux Cave, 2, 7
Latin, 12, 20
Lavillenie, Renaud, 129
Le Corbusier, 76
Le Pen, Marine, 97, 102
Leipzig, Battle of, 57, 59, 60
Lenglen, Suzanne, 127
Leo III, Pope, 19
Leonardo da Vinci, 32
Libya, 107
Louis IX, Saint, 27, 30, 31
Louis the Pious, 21, 22
Louis VI, 30
Louis VII, 27, 30, 31
Louis XI, 38
Louis XIII, 41, 47, 48, 49
Louis XIV, 43, 44, 45, 47, 48, 49,
     111, 120
Louis XV, 48
Louis XVI, 48, 50, 52, 58, 59
Louis XVIII, 61, 62, 68
Louis-Philippe, King, 63, 64, 68,
     69
Lugdunum (Lyon), 11, 12, 15
Lully, Jean-Baptiste, 45
Lumière, Auguste and Louis, 124
Lutetia, 11
Luxembourg, 4
Maastricht Treaty (1992), 94,
     101, 103
Macron, Emmanuel, 98, 100,
     101, 102, 110, 112
Madame de Pompadour, 48
Manet, Édouard, 123
Marat, Jean-Paul, 58
Marie Antoinette, 48
Marne, Battle of the, 81
Marseille, 11, 103, 127
Marshall Plan, 83
Martinique, 104
Massilia (Marseille), 11
Mazarin, Cardinal, 43
Mbappé, Kylian, 129
Megalithic Stones, 7
Merkel, Angela, 102
Merovech, 16
Merovingian dynasty, 16, 18, 22
Metz, 69
Migration, 15, 113
Missi Dominici, 20
Mitterrand, François, 93, 102,
     111
Molière, 45, 123
Mona Lisa, 32
Monet, Claude, 70, 121
Monnet, Jean, 84, 91
Mont Beuvray, 5
Montaigne, Michel de, 33
Montesquieu, Charles, 51
Morocco, 104
Moulin Rouge, 71, 121

Nantes, 36, 49
Napoleon III. *See* Bonaparte,
     Louis Napoleon
Napoleonic Code, 59, 61, 121
Napoleonic Wars, 59, 60
National Rally, 97, 101, 102
NATO, 88, 105, 106, 107
Nazi Germany, 77
Nelson, Horatio, 58
Neolithic era, 2
Netherlands, 4
Normandy, 31, 78, 81, 82
North America, 105, 111
Oil Crises, 92
Organisation Internationale de
     la Francophonie (OIF), 105
Orléans, Siege of, 28, 39
Ouagadougou, Burkina Faso,
     112
Pacific, 104
Palaeolithic era, 1, 7
Paris, 11, 22, 23, 34, 36, 52, 66,
     67, 70, 76, 77, 78, 109
Paris Agreement (2015), 103
Paris Commune, 66, 67, 80, 81
Paris Fashion Week, 99, 122
Paris Metro bombings (1995),
     103
Peace of Alais, 42
Pérec, Marie-José, 128
Pétain, Marshal Philippe, 74, 77
Pétain, Philippe, 80, 81
Philip I, 23, 30
Philip II Augustus, 24, 27, 30, 31
Philip IV, 30, 31
Philip VI, 38, 39
Piaf Edith, 124
Picasso, Pablo, 76
Platini, Michel, 128
Poitiers, Battle of, 27
Popular Front, The, 75, 81, 101
Prost, Alain, 128
Protestant, 34, 36, 49
Proust, Marcel, 71, 105
Rabelais, François, 33
Racine, Jean, 45
Raymond IV of Toulouse, 26
Reign of Terror, 54, 58, 59
Reims, 17, 28, 30, 39, 127
Remigius, Saint, 17
Renaissance, The, 32, 39
Renoir, Pierre-Auguste, 70
Revolution of 1848, 64, 65, 69
Richard the Lionheart, 27
Richelieu, Cardinal, 41, 42, 48,
     49, 121
Riner, Teddy, 129
Robert II, 23, 30
Robespierre, Maximilien, 53, 54,
     58
Rocroi, Battle of, 49
Roman Conquest, 6, 9
Rome, 9, 10, 128
Rousseau, Jean Jacques, 51, 121
Russia, 60, 69
Saint Helena, 60
Sarkozy, Nicolas, 102, 107, 111

Saxons, 21
Second Empire 1852, 65, 66, 68,
     69
Second Republic, 65, 68, 69
Sedan, Battle of, 69
Senegal, 104, 112
Single European Act (1986), 93
Soissons, Battle of, 16
Somme, Battle of the, 74
Spanish Succession, War of the,
     45, 49
St. Bartholomew's Day
     Massacre, 34
Strasbourg, 91, 103
Sun King. *See* Louis XIV
Surrealist movement, 76
Switzerland, 4, 34
Syagrius, 16
Tennis Court Oath, 53
The #MeToo movement, 100
Thiers, Adolphe, 68, 80
Third Republic, 66, 67, 68, 69,
     70, 75, 80
Thirty Glorious Years, 84, 92
Thirty Years' War, 49
Tolbiac, Battle of, 16
Toulouse, 103
Tour de France, 122, 128
Tours, Battle of, 22
Trafalgar, Battle of, 58, 60
Treaty of Arras, 39
Treaty of Paris, 31
Treaty of Versailles, 74, 81
Treaty on European Union. *See*
     Maastricht Treaty
Trente Glorieuses. *See* Thirty
     Glorious Years
Truffaut, François, 106, 124
Tunisia, 104
UNESCO, 100, 122
United Nations, 105, 106, 107
Valois dynasty, 27, 37, 38, 40
Vassy, Massacre of, 34
Veil, Simone, 91
Vercingetorix, 7, 8, 9, 10, 15
Verdun, Battle of, 74
Versailles, 43, 44, 48, 49, 59, 66,
     68, 80, 91, 120
Vichy France, 77
Vietnam, 104, 112, 113
Viking invasions, 22
Visigoths, 15, 17
Voltaire, 51, 121, 123
Vouillé, Battle of, 17
Waterloo, Battle of, 60
West Francia, 22
William the Conqueror, 31
World Trade Organization, 110
World War I, 70, 73, 80, 81
World War II, 77, 80, 81, 82, 83,
     90, 91, 111
Yamoussoukro, Côte d'Ivoire,
     112
Yellow Vests, 99, 103, 110
Zidane, Zinedine, 128

THE STATE EMBLEM OF FRANCE - www.de-academic.com
THE FLAG OF FRANCE - www.pixelstalk.net
THE LOCATION OF FRANCE – Public domain, via Wikimedia Commons
THE LASCAUX CAVE PAINTINGS - EUX, Public domain, via Wikimedia Commons
MEGALITHIC STONES IN THE VILLAGE OF CARNAC (BRITTANY) - alex-guillaume unsplash
GAUL FORTIFICATION SITE IN BIBRACTE (MONT BEUVRAY) - www.alchetron.com
ROMAN EMPEROR JULIUS CAESAR - nemanja-peric unsplash
CAESAR'S "COMMENTARII DE BELLO GALLICO" - Public domain, via Wikimedia Commons
MODERN RECREATION OF ROMAN ALESIA FORTIFICATIONS - Prosopee, via Wikimedia Commons
MAP OF ROMAN GAUL (C. 55-50 BC) - www.shorthistory.org
A ROMAN SITE IN LUGDUNUM (MODERN LYON) - www.topworldimages.com
CLOVIS I LEADING THE FRANKS TO VICTORY IN THE TOLBIAC BATTLE - Ary Scheffer, Public domain, via Wikimedia Commons
MAP OF THE MEROVINGIAN KINGDOMS - Rudric, via Wikimedia Commons
POPE LEO III CROWNING CHARLEMAGNE - Public domain, via Wikimedia Commons
THE PALACE SCHOOL AT AACHEN (AIX-LA-CHAPELLE) 792-805 - www.artsy.net
THE CORONATION OF PHILIP II AUGUSTUS - Bibliothèque nationale de France, Public domain, via Wikimedia Commons
THE EIGHT PHASES OF 'THE SONG OF ROLAND' - Simon Marmion, Public domain, via Wikimedia Commons
MEDIEVAL MANUSCRIPT DEPICTING THE SIEGE OF JERUSALEM (1099) - Public domain, via Wikimedia Commons
JOAN OF ARC ENTERS ORLÉANS (1429) - Jean-Jacques Scherrer, Public domain, via Wikimedia Commons
THE CHÂTEAU DE FONTAINEBLEAU - Draceane, via Wikimedia Commons
THE MASSACRE OF VASSY (1562) - Hogenberg, Public domain, via Wikimedia Commons
CATHERINE DE' MEDICI - www.bjws.blogspot.com
HENRY IV SIGNING THE EDICT OF NANTES - www.magnoliabox.com
CARDINAL RICHELIEU (ARMAND JEAN DU PLESSIS)- Public domain, via Wikimedia Commons
LA ROCHELLE DURING THE 1628 SIEGE - PHGCOM, Public domain, via Wikimedia Commons
LOUIS XIV (THE SUN KING) - Hyacinthe Rigaud, Public domain, via Wikimedia Commons
VERSAILLES PALACE GROUNDS - ToucanWings, via Wikimedia Commons
MOLIÈRE IN CLASSICAL DRESS - Nicolas Mignard, Public domain, via Wikimedia Commons
THE ENCYCLOPÉDIE OF THE SCIENCES, ARTS, AND CRAFTS - www.sothebys.com
MAXIMILIEN ROBESPIERRE LED THE 'REIGN OF TERROR' - Unidentified painter, via Wikimedia Commons
KING LOUIS XVI EXECUTED ON 21ST JANUARY 1793 - Public domain, via Wikimedia Commons
EMPEROR NAPOLEON BONAPARTE (1803) - Andrea Appiani, Public domain, via Wikimedia Commons
NAPOLEON'S DEFEAT AT THE BATTLE OF LEIPZIG (1813) - Alexander von Sauerweid, Public domain, via Wikimedia Commons
RETURN OF THE BOURBON MONARCHY UNDER LOUIS XVIII - François Gérard, Public domain, via Wikimedia Commons
A SCENE FROM THE JULY REVOLUTION OF 1830 - www.studymateriall.com
LOUIS-PHILIPPE (THE "CITIZEN KING") - Franz Xaver Winterhalter, Public domain, via Wikimedia Commons
NAPOLEON III SURRENDERS TO WILHELM I AND CROWN PRINCE FREDERICK - Public domain, via Wikimedia Commons
A BARRICADE IN THE PARIS COMMUNE, MARCH 18, 1871 - Musée Carnavalet, Public domain, via Wikimedia Commons
THE EIFFEL TOWER COMPLETED IN 1889 - Benh LIEU SONG, via Wikimedia Commons
PAINTING BY CLAUDE MONET 'SPRINGTIME' - Public domain, via Wikimedia Commons
ALFRED DREYFUS IN CAPTIVITY ON DEVIL'S ISLAND 1898 - Georgfotoart, Public domain, via Wikimedia Commons
GERMAN SOLDIERS IN THE TRENCHES, JULY 1916 - www.smithsonianmag.com
SUFFERING AND WOES OF THE GREAT DEPRESSION 1930S - www.flickr.com
LE CORBUSIER SYNONYMOUS WITH THE 'ART DECO' MOVEMENT - www.tpsearchtool.com
GERMAN SOLDIERS ON THE CHAMPS ÉLYSÉES ON 14 JUNE 1940 - Bundesarchiv, via Wikimedia Commons
ALLIED INVASION PLANS AND GERMAN POSITIONS IN NORMANDY - Public domain, via Wikimedia Commons
PLAQUE WHERE JEAN MONNET LIVED AS COMMISSIONER FROM 1946-1952 - Public domain, via Wikimedia Commons
FRENCH PATROL IN ORLEANSVILLE (CHLEF) ALGERIA IN 1957 - Facebook Group, Public domain, via Wikimedia Commons
FRANCE AND ALGERIA'S SIGNING OF THE EVIAN ACCORDS ON 18 MARCH 1962 - www.rfi.fr
CHARLES DE GAULLE BACK TO POWER IN 1958 - www.scmp.com
MAY 1968 DEMONSTRATIONS IN BORDEAUX - Tangopaso, Public domain, via Wikimedia Commons
PRESIDENT FRANÇOIS MITTERRAND IN 1983 - www.wikispooks.com
THE SIGNING OF THE MAASTRICHT TREATY IN 1992 - www.cvce.eu
IMMIGRATION POLARISED IN MODERN TIMES - www.europapress.es
MARINE LE PEN LEADER OF THE NATIONAL RALLY - www.britannica.com
SCENE AT THE SHOOTING AT CHARLIE HEBDO'S OFFICE (2015) - Thierry Caro _Jérémie Hartmann, via Wikimedia Commons
YELLOW VEST PROTESTS AGAINST MACRON'S POLICIES 2018 - Thomas Bresson, via Wikimedia Commons
EMMANUEL MACRON FRANCE'S PRESIDENT SINCE 2017 - www.president.gov.ua, via Wikimedia Commons
MAP OF THE FRANCOPHONE WORLD - Jpthefish, via Wikimedia Commons
GENERAL ASSEMBLY OF THE UNITED NATIONS - azugaldia, via Wikimedia Commons
NATO EMBLEM - Public domain, via Wikimedia Commons
MAP OF EUROPEAN UNION MEMBERS - Robert Laymont, via Wikimedia Commons
THE PARIS AGREEMENT, ADOPTED IN 2015 - UNclimatechange from Bonn, Germany, via Wikimedia Commons

Iceland Through the Ages (2024) ISBN: 9786197742435	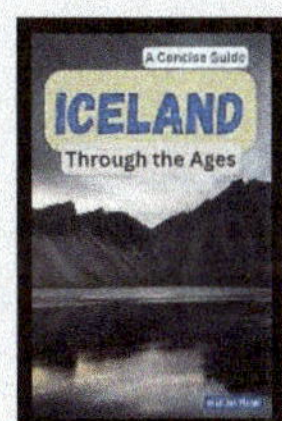	**26 Tales of Humanities Trials** (2023) ISBN 9786199249482	
Simple Treasures in Bulgaria (2008) ISBN 9780955984907		**I'm Bad at Poems** (2022) ISBN 9786199249420	
Wales Through the Ages (2023) ISBN 9786197742336		**Redemption of Love** (2023) ISBN 9786199249406	
100 Essential Recipes from Bulgaria (2011) ISBN 9781447702603		**Malta Through the Ages (2024)** ISBN 9786197742350	
North Macedonia Through the Ages (2023) ISBN 9786197742251		**Cyprus Through the Ages** (2023) ISBN 9786197742220	

www.ingramcontent.com/pod-product-compliance
Lightning Source LLC
LaVergne TN
LVHW050540200726
843506LV00001B/33